"ACERBIC AND FRANK . . .
Her storytelling ability shines through in poignant yet lurid tales like that of a friend whose mother was an alcoholic, or her own horrible experiences of betrayal and rejection at summer camp."
—*Creative Loafing* (Atlanta, GA)

"An anthem to self-reliance . . . Cho has met and mingled with a sweeping variety of characters in the course of her thirty-two years, from drag queens, punk rockers, and drug dealers to film producers, television stars, and Bill and Hillary Clinton."
—*Vancouver Columbian* (WA)

"All the Korean family stories, dark days of adolescence, pill-addled comedy benders, and infuriating television show development meetings are in here, along with deeper insight into Cho's anguished but very amusing mind. Careening between her reflections of a painful childhood and her ultimate acceptance of herself, warts and all, Cho celebrates the many gay men or, as she calls them, angels, that pulled her out of her own hell while still making catty remarks along the way."
—*Instinct* (North Hollywood, CA)

"Fierce, funny, and wise . . . Though loosely based on her critically acclaimed stage show and smash box-office film of the same name, this book is a wholly original work, with an inspiring message for anyone who has ever been told they are not good enough, smart enough, pretty enough, or just not enough, period."
—*Asian Pages*

I'M THE

ONE

THAT

I WANT

MARGARET CHO

BALLANTINE BOOKS • NEW YORK

A Ballantine Book
Published by The Ballantine Publishing Group

www.ballantinebooks.com

Library of Congress Catalog Card Number: 2002090327

ISBN 0-345-44014-5

Cover design by Min Choi
Cover photo by Mark Veltman

Manufactured in the United States of America

First Hardcover Edition: May 2001
First Trade Paperback Edition: May 2002

10 9 8 7 6 5 4 3 2

This book is dedicated to my parents
Young Hie and Seung Hoon Cho.

I'M THE ONE
THAT I WANT

1

ALONE, STEALING AND WAVING

I was born on December 5, 1968, at Children's Hospital in San Francisco.

My mother says, "You were so small. Just like this!" and she makes a fist and shakes it. "You grow so much! Can you imagine?! Just tiny baby!"

I can't imagine being that small. It must have been the one time I didn't worry about my weight. At 5 pounds, 6 ounces, I was the Calista Flockhart of the newborn set.

My earliest memories are mostly unpleasant. The first thing I can truly remember is standing in front of a sink in my footie pajamas being berated by a bunch of old people. They must have been my grandparents. I couldn't wash my face, and they were making fun of me.

"Dirty face! Dirty face!" They all laughed and then started coughing.

My mother was about to leave me with them and, presumably, was hiding her guilt behind my inability to wash my face. I was so small I had to stand on a stool to reach the sink. I had a tremendous fear that if I immersed my face in the water I would not return, I would drown, or water would go up my nose, or I would somehow be hijacked.

I also feared that if I took my eyes off my mother, she would leave. And she did. My parents had a talent for leaving me places when I was very young. This had to do with immigration difficulties, living in San Francisco in 1968 and not being hippies, LBJ, men on the moon, and having their first child while being totally unprepared for reality. My father didn't know how to break it to my mother that he was to be deported three days after I was born, so he conveniently avoided the subject. He didn't lie; he simply withheld the truth and at the last minute, he left her holding the bag. Or me, as it were.

In my parents' colorfully woven mythology, that was the one corner of the tapestry they carefully concealed. Knowing I probably wouldn't remember, they kept it to themselves. But I did remember, perhaps not actual events but colors and shapes and feelings. The insides of planes, the smell of fuel, unfamiliar arms, crying and crying. Wanting my mom but not having the words, not even knowing what I wanted.

When questioned about it now, my mother spills forth resentment and regret. "Can you imagine mommy?! Oh! It was so terrible. I have to take care of you by myself and Daddy go back to Korea and then I have to send you to Korea and all this you only three days! Can you imagine?! Oh! I hate Daddy!"

My father says cryptically that he was testing the waters, scoping out the situation, whatever that means.

It was all an unfortunate turn of events, but in the spirit of my birthplace, I learned that if I couldn't be with the one I loved, I would love the one I was with. I was one, and already somewhat of a slut.

I loved lots of stewardesses, and lots of old people. When I was reunited with my parents, my mother showed me pictures of an ancient, bony woman in a white Korean *ham-bok*. "She was your auntie and she take care of you when you baby. She love you soooo much! She just die. She is in heaven. But she take so good care of you. She love you soo much!!!!!" I believed she was dead because in the picture she looked like a skeleton, even though her wide smile made her kind and human. Some infantile, suckling part of me remembered her face and I wanted to weep with baby grief.

My mother's father also died around this time in 1970. For some reason, her family did not let her know of his passing until long after the funeral. She sat on her bed holding one of those blue air-mail letters that is also its own envelope. *Par avion.* She was crying, letting her tears fall on the blue paper and smear the ink, odd Korean letters looking like a bunch of sticks that had fallen on the page. I was alarmed by her sadness—I hadn't witnessed it before. I jumped on the bed and wrapped my small arms around her and said, "Don't cry Mommy. I will be your mommy now." I was fully aware of how cute I was being. I was destined for a career in show business.

Even then, I loved television, and my favorite thing to watch was the coverage of the Watergate scandal. I'd put my fist in my mouth and then smear my hand across the TV screen, watching the saliva make rainbow tracks all over Richard Nixon's face.

We lived in a little apartment with my aunt and uncle on Washington Street. It was nice going from having no parents, to suddenly having four. My mother would make me special outfits—red wooly jackets with pillbox hats, just like Jackie O—and we'd all go to the park, where I would cry whenever I saw a dog.

My aunt and uncle ran a convenience store on Nob Hill, and sometimes after nursery school, my mother would drop me there so she could run errands. I became enamored of a product they sold called Binaca Blast, which tasted like candy but also like medicine. Drop by drop, I wanted to consume the entire bottle of icy freshness, feeling it explode on my tongue. One time I had slugged down the contents of my aunt's bottle laying next to the cash register, then I reached up to the display and pulled a new one right off the metal rod. I threw its cardboard package into the garbage can and indulged my minty jones until my mother came and picked me up.

The next day, when I was dropped off at the store, the tension was so thick you could cut it with a knife. My aunt called me up to the back room for a "talk."

In the room there was a bare lightbulb swinging above my head. I was only three, but I knew an interrogation when I saw one.

"I know that you took that breath freshener. I want you to know that is 'stealing.' If you ask me, I will give you anything you want. But ask me first. Don't steal. Stealing is bad. Okay?"

"But I wasn't stealing."

She looked at me hard.

"Oh really? Now, it's okay. I'm not mad. But just don't do it again."

She gave me a hug and sent me back downstairs. I looked on the table, and there it was—the crumpled up cardboard packaging of Binaca Blast confirming my guilt.

The lesson I learned that day was to destroy all the evidence. As I lay in my crib, which was much too small for me, barely accommodating my head as I angled my feet up to the top of the bars, I played the incident over and over in my mind. I saw myself getting the Binaca Blast, tearing it out of the package, carefully gathering up the cardboard and the plastic, carrying it outside, looking around to make sure I had no witnesses, then dumping it in the trash can down the street, and running back into the store to enjoy the adrenaline of getting away with the goods. The spooky thing is I would always wake up in the morning with minty fresh breath.

I was enrolled in Notre Dame Nursery School, which was run by nuns. Being a known hustler did not win me much favor with the sisters. Most days, I found myself in Mother Superior's office for my involvement in daycare crimes such as fingerpainting my neighbor and crawling around on the floor with an older man, a boy of five, during nap time.

Mother Superior's chambers were dark and cool, and even though the nuns would threaten me all day long with being sent there, nothing ever happened when I arrived. Mother Superior would just nod her wimpled head and smile up at me through her glasses like Ben Franklin.

We had a Christmas pageant, and all the kids in the school were involved in a grand-finale number, singing a song for the Virgin Mary. The nuns kept saying during rehearsal, "When you see your parents out in the audience, don't wave. Do you hear me? Don't wave. If you wave, Jesus will be mad you messed up His song. Don't wave. If you wave, you will go to Hell. Don't wave. Don't wave."

When I went out on the stage, I saw my mom and my aunt in the crowd and they started to wave wildly! What could I do? I was having a moral dilemma. I kept seeing the nun's face in my mind's eye *("Don't wave . . . don't wave . . .")*, but here was my mom and my aunt doing just that! I couldn't leave them hanging! In slow motion, my hand went up. It was like it wasn't even attached to me. I couldn't control it. It just started to move back and forth, and before I knew it, I was waving. My partner-in-crime, the boy of five, saw what I was doing and was not about to let me lead the revolution all by myself. He started to wave at his parents in the front row, who of course waved back, setting off another little kid and his parents and another and another. Pretty soon, the entire audience and all the kids on stage were waving at each other like we were on a float! Unfortunately, this was no parade. It was total Christmas-pageant anarchy and no one was even sure what to sing anymore and the nuns rushed us off the stage.

I thought I would be in trouble, but then when the pageant was over, we were let off for winter break, and by the time we got back, nobody remembered what happened or who waved first or anything. I was a bit disappointed that it was forgotten so easily, but I learned something very important that day: When you are on a stage and you wave, people wave back. This information would become very important for me later on.

My father was not around for a lot of my early childhood. He was still in Korea trying to get a visa or something. When he'd come back into town, I would welcome him by taking him into my arms and throwing up all over his back.

We didn't have a car back then, so my mom and I took the bus everywhere. She says I was very friendly to people, always saying "hi" first, smiling, making amicable conversation, all this glad-handing at only four years of age.

"The people in the bus, sometimes don't say 'hi,' or anything back. Sometimes they just look down! How can be? That so mean, mean people. You always so nice, saying 'Hello!' and smile and smile and so charming! Bad, bad people."

I don't think I was put off by people not responding to my gregariousness, as my behavior was not entirely without self-interest. I'd learned early on that if you smiled at people, it increased your chances of candy, as these were the days when you could still accept it from strangers. If they did not smile back, they did not have candy, so I moved on.

When I was five, my brother was born, and everything changed. He was the cutest thing in the world, and we kissed him so much he was smelly. We moved to a house in the Sunset District and our grandparents came from Korea to take care of us. I started elementary school at Dudley Stone in the Haight, and would come home on the bus in the afternoon and help my grandmother take care of the baby.

My parents started running a snack bar in the Japantown Bowling Alley and my brother and I got big, eating hamburgers every day.

2

MARCO AND PATTY'S MOM

For kindergarten and first and second grades, I went to Dudley Stone School in the Haight. Haight Street was still coming down from the '60s, and it was a dirty and burned-out place during the '70s. Highlights of these years: I put some seeds on a sponge and pushed toothpicks into an avocado and farted in the cardboard playhouse.

I had a boyfriend named Marco Picoli, and he and I would go to his house on Saturdays. On one of these visits we went to the corner store forty-one times. He was the only straight man I ever met who liked to shop. Actually, I can't be sure he was straight, since I had no way of confirming it back then. I had procured a dollar that day from my parents and first we had trouble deciding what to get and then trying to return the candy we bought because we were dissatisfied with our choices. They wouldn't let us exchange the bubblegum cigar for wax lips. We even had the receipt!

He had a doll that was white and then when you flipped it over it was black, and for some reason, it would make us scream laughing. He moved to New York after first grade, and I never saw him again. Over time I've realized that this was probably my best relationship.

There was a girl who lived next door to us who was my friend when we were at home but not at school, a kind of separation of church and state. Her name was Patty and she had a big German shepherd named Zuzu who followed her everywhere. We were only around eight or nine, but she was already sexually active, making it with the dirty neighborhood boys in the parking garage at the end of our block. She wore very short dresses and had an overbite like some '70s groupie. One time we were in her backyard and she took a shit in the flower box and Zuzu came up and ate the turds. She and Zuzu were so nonchalant and synchronized about it that I imagined this to be a regular thing. I told my mom, and she never let me go over there again.

Patty's mom was an alcoholic. She wore a white slip and an orange robe all day, smoking More's and drinking Beefeater gin out of a jelly jar in the front room. Their house was exactly like ours, the same layout, the rooms in the same order, but it could not have been more different.

My parents kept the same bottle of Cutty Sark for nearly a decade. Nobody in our family drank. They were crazy in their own repressed Korean way, but it didn't have to do with alcohol.

Patty's mom was mysterious to me, hunched over in the front room that was just like ours, curtains drawn to keep out the noonday sun, slowly drinking and smoking and staring at the blank space in front of her. What was she looking at? What did she see?

Patty's Uncle Will lived with them, too. He was an uptight but friendly bachelor, with geeky, black plastic glasses and crisp, white short-sleeve button-down oxfords, forever carrying bags of groceries into the soon-to-be haunted house.

Sometime after the Flower Box Incident, I saw Will standing on the front steps. He was holding the glasses away from his eyes and crying. When he took his glasses off, he took his face with them. My mom told me that Patty's mom had died the night before and Patty and Will were moving away.

That same week, the Shroud of Turin made the cover of National

Geographic. I would lie awake all night thinking about Patty's mom, wrapped in the Shroud of Turin, coming into my room and getting me. I thought of her long, blue-white fingers curling around my shoulders, her haggy face a mask of sadness and regret. She wore only pajamas. She was always tired. I remembered her unscrewing the metal caps of the tall gin bottles, the long ash of her cigarette breaking into the big, deep ashtray already filled with brown, skinny butts. She died in her front room that was just like ours. She'd had enough of the dark, the smoke, the booze, the crazy daughter, weird Will, the shit-eating dog, that bathrobe, everything. So she just died.

I hadn't known anyone before who had died, so the whole process was terrifying to me. How could someone die right in their house? Didn't that mean the place would be cursed forever? I wanted to tell the new family that moved in, but they were never friendly enough for me to want to volunteer that kind of information. They were Chinese, and very distant. They had two teenage boys and a big chow dog and they all hated my brother and me.

A couple of years later, I had taken up cigarettes and was smoking out the window of my bathroom. I would smoke and then shower directly afterward to cleanse the air. (This was before I realized it just spread the smell out into the hallway.) I heard a knock on the window of the house next door. I looked over and saw the curtains had been drawn back, revealing the naked torso of one of the boys. He held out his hard cock with one hand and pulled back the curtain with the other. Then, as if that weren't enough, he used his elbow to keep the curtains back and flipped me off with his free hand. It was totally gymnastic and totally upsetting. I threw the lit cigarette into their yard and hoped it would start a fire.

That house was haunted all right.

I'd often see those boys working on their Trans Am in the afternoons, and neither of them ever acknowledged me.

I grew up, left home, got famous, nearly drank myself to death, and, for a time, became the very image of Patty's mom. Except I didn't have curtains to draw, so the living room would be flooded with a piercing light that burned holes in my brain. I tried to sleep as much of the day as I could to avoid the unbearable morning cheerfulness of my sunny, Hollywood Hills bungalow. My pajamas stayed on all the time, and I had the same hunch, the same sick expression, the same dead-eyed stare. I should have died, too, but I didn't. For some reason, someone or something or Jesus rolled the rock away from the front of my house and I emerged, Shroud of Turin falling away at my feet, and I, newly risen from the dead, went to Melrose and bought some fabulous new clothes to replace it.

3

BRAVERY

I have always thought of myself as brave. I have also always thought there would be people, boys especially, who would admire me, look at me, fawn over me. And there were—until I was eight and did two terrible, unforgivable things in the third grade. They happened within a period of two weeks. The first was during a bell rehearsal for the Christmas program. We were all handed very expensive, delicate, rare brass bells with which to play "Greensleeves" and we were warned and warned again and threatened and warned some more about the value of the bells. We were made to wear cotton gloves so that we would not get our fingerprints on the precious fucking bells. As I was putting my gloves on, bell stuck between my upper arm and my side, I dropped the bell and it shattered on the ground. It was an E flat or C sharp or something definitely irreplaceable, so when the choir sang "What child is this . . ." the word *child* came without musical accompaniment, naked, the brutal reminder to me and all the rest of Grade Three of my grievous act.

Some time later, the worse of the two incidents occurred. During another bell rehearsal, as I had no bell to play, I sat in the back of class fidgeting and counting my fingers or something. I really had to pee, so I went to the front of the class and said to the teacher, "I have to pee." And she said, "Just wait." I returned to the back of class and the business of idling, when I was hit with an urgent, desperate need to pee that would not wait. I had to do it. After the rehearsal, half-midget perennial spinster Miss Cinnamon said, "Okay, you can go now." I answered, quite wittily I must say, "I already did."

I think that I was so used to horror, my little life had already endured such atrocities, that I was unfazed by my "accident." I sat there in thoroughly wet, itchy pants with a pool of urine underneath me, cultivating a "been there, done that" attitude. This highly disturbed the teachers, and when they asked if I wanted to go home and change, if I wanted my mom to come get me, if there was someone they could call—I looked down at my pee-splattered Buster Browns and said, "No. Why would you want to do that?" and went off to play kickball. And I thought nobody had wanted me on their team before.

The taunts and the teasing came later. At this point, I think everyone was too afraid of me to make fun of me. They treated me like Damien in *The Omen*, as if one look of my evil eye would render them incontinent. The spell was broken soon enough. I was the pariah of the schoolyard, shunned as if I had the floor-length beard and long, curly nails of the unwashed untouchables of India. To me, "recess" meant "riot," the time of day I stood between massive groups of eight-year-olds fighting over whether I should be called the Bell Breaker or the Pee Girl. I was stoic, silent, nonviolent even back then. I didn't pay attention. But I stayed at that same school for five more years, which is forever when you are a kid, and I must admit, *it wore me down*. I think I lost something there—an interior brightness. The luster and the silver lining and the Tootsie Roll center and the brave one in me went far underground, now surfacing, twisted, perverted, deformed, with a dowager's hump and a bad nervous tic, but tougher still.

My family went to church every Sunday, at first to the one by Stonestown, where my grandfather led the services, and later to the big Korean Methodist Church on Powell Street that was in the middle of Chinatown. Sometimes big Chinese funeral processions would lurch slowly down the street. There would be a brass band made up of men dressed like they were in the military, playing solemnly as they marched by. Then there'd be a black convertible, with an enormous black-and-white photo of the deceased, bordered with black bands to signify the departure into the afterlife, attached to the windshield. The hearse would follow, its windows crammed with flowers behind a white curtain, hiding the mysterious gleaming casket. I wanted to hold my breath as it went by. I thought if I got too close and looked into the hearse, a bony hand would emerge from it and drag me inside. Carloads of mourners trailed behind, and they all moved so slowly, it seemed like it would take forever to get where they were going. But it hardly mattered. There is lots of time when you are dead. These processions made me dread and look forward to Sunday at the same time.

The church services were held in Korean, so a massive Sunday school system existed to accommodate all the exclusively English-speaking kids. It was broken down into two groups, the baby classes with Jesus coloring books and the Methodist Youth Foundation, which was for the teenagers who cut class and went into Chinatown to smoke cigarettes and talk about what they'd done Saturday night. When they did go to class, it was like a cool "rap" session, involving young pastors getting out their acoustic guitars and talking about the "downer" of premarital sex.

They *hated* me there. Everyone. From the babies all the way to the teenagers. Maybe the teachers and the young pastor didn't, because they'd spend time trying to protect me and involve me in some activities, the same ones the other kids would try to exclude me from. I don't think anyone could have been more hated. School was bad enough, but now it seemed like the whole world was a hostile place.

This was the '80s and I was twelve, a preteen with a Dorothy Hamill haircut and braces. Hated. Hated. Hated. I tried to ignore it, spending summers away with cousins who lived in magical Glendale, where I would sit by their swimming pool reading a waterlogged copy of *Seventeen*. Lori Laughlin set the beauty standard, and as I looked at her, my troubles would melt away. "Someday I will be seventeen . . ." But the thing that I couldn't admit to myself was that I was really wishing "Someday . . . I will be *white*."

Whenever I read those magazines and tried to plug into the teenage fantasy they were selling, I couldn't see myself at all. I studied those pictures and the TV and movies like *Little Darlings* over and over. Then in the mirror I would be confronted with the awful reality that I was *not that*. It was almost too much to bear.

My Koreanness, my "otherness," embarrassed me. When I had school projects that required the use of glue, a product my family had little need or money for, my mother would substitute leftover rice. My face would get all red and I would shake and stammer, "Why can't we have American glue!! I hate you, Mommy!!!!" Then I would stamp my feet up the stairs and throw my hot face down on my canopy bed.

Since I didn't really have friends who I was not related to, and the kids that were cruelest to me were other Koreans, my entire world was an exercise in not belonging. The answer seemed to lie in being white, so in my fantasy life, I chose to be Lori Laughlin. In my mind, I got ready for dances, wearing only a neat white towel wrapped under my arms, spraying myself with Love's Baby Soft, wiping a cotton ball soaked in 10-0-6 lotion over my troublesome T-zone, lining my big, big eyes with Aziza by Prince Matchabelli, putting on a long, ruffled denim skirt with a petticoat underneath and then a puffy-sleeved blouse with a big ruffle forming a V on my ample but not slutty chest. Then finally, I'd let my naturally curly chestnut hair fall across my narrow shoulders, pulling it up close to my head with red oval barrettes. The only time the fantasy would change would be if I decided to be Charlene Tilton instead of Lori Laughlin, but this occurred less frequently because I read in *Teen Beat* that Charlene took forty-five minutes to blow-dry her hair, which even then I found unreasonable.

I usually never got to the dance, because my fantasies were all about getting ready, looking a certain way, about not being me. How sad to use such a rich and vibrant imagination to dream about *grooming*, and not only that, but *grooming someone else*.

Sometimes, I would get so caught up in the fantasy that I would actually go to the dance, but since I'd never been to one yet, that image was rather muddled. I'd end up slow-dancing to Air Supply with the cutest guy in my grade, Steve Goldberg, a hot Jewish kid with blonde hair and a huge ass. Steve was relentlessly mean to me, perhaps because he knew I had a crush on him, but he was also in his own pain because of his big behind. Once, on a field trip, he made all the kids in the class say "Hi Margaret" to a big golden retriever as they walked by. "Hey everybody, say hi to Margaret. She's a dog! Get it?!" I wasn't offended. I always thought dogs were beautiful. It hurt me only because it was *meant* to, but it was nothing compared to the treatment I got at church.

It started with my name. I was born Moran Cho. Moran is a Korean name, meaning peony flower, a plant that blooms even in the harshest winter. My father gave me this thoughtful, unusual name without the knowledge that someday the kids I grew up with would use it against me. It started when I was around twelve, not at school, but at church.

"MORON!! YOU ARE NOTHIN' BUT A MORON!!!" They said my name every chance they got.

"Excuse me, but MORON didn't pass the basket this way."

"Hey! I have my hand up. You can't see me past MORON'S fat head."

"May I be moved? I don't want to sit next to MORON!"

"Jesus loves everyone, even MORON."

It was stupid, but it hurt my feelings so much. Especially since the main perpetrators had once been close friends of mine.

Lotte and Connie Park were the daughters of my parents' best friends. During the previous summer vacation, I had spent many days at their house in San Bruno. We listened to Michael Jackson's *Off the Wall*. We went down the hill to Kmart and I bought my first pair of designer jeans. We watched *Creature Features* until we got too scared and had to change the channel to *Saturday Night Live*, where we'd laugh our asses off at Steve Martin doing King Tut.

They told me their parents fought all night long, but when they prayed to God to make them stop, it got quiet. They said they were afraid their parents were going to get a divorce. I was scared that was going to happen to me, too. We were kids of the '80s, when divorce and nuclear war loomed large. We were afraid of being abandoned by our parents, yet excited at the possibility of peace in our homes and spending our weekends with dads we never saw as long as our parents stayed together. We also had nightmares of radioactive fallout and hoped that we'd get stuck in a bomb shelter with a cute guy.

Connie had a tendency to have sties, which gave her eyes the bubbly look of a pop-eyed goldfish, but she was thin and confident, which made her condition seem oddly attractive. Lotte looked like a Korean Genie Francis, which was exciting as this was the time when *General Hospital* ruled the airwaves—there was even a song about it, parodying the plotlines and the scandalous characters, and we'd call up KFRC and request it over and over again.

We'd commiserate about our piano teachers, the strange, old white people who would come into our homes and sit next to us as we hammered out "Close to You" on the keys. Those lessons were the one luxury my family could afford, and my brother and I suffered through them for years. Lotte and Connie would make me howl with laughter at the tales of their teacher, who would use the bathroom for up to half an hour, and help herself to Sanka in the kitchen. "Best cup I ever made . . ."

I don't know why it was so funny. Maybe because this was the first time anybody seemed to *understand* me. Those girls made me feel so much less alone in the world, which made their betrayal particularly painful.

Lotte and Connie had a cousin, a shy, awkward girl named Ronny, who started going to our church. She had two older brothers who were really good-looking, with glossy, black feathered hair and tan, hard bodies, which made her popular by proxy. I was friendly to her at first, not knowing that she was to be my replacement.

One day Lotte came up to Ronny and me as we chit-chatted in the church parking lot. She looked at Ronny with a knowing glance and said, "Oh, I see you've met MORON!!!" They both started laughing hysterically and I tried to be a good sport, accepting it as some healthy ribbing among friends, even though my face got red and a knot grew in my throat. The two girls walked off and joined Connie, who was nursing a sty the size of a golf ball. They didn't speak to me again for the rest of the day, which was suspicious, but I tried to ignore it.

I went home and looked in the mirror to see if there was something wrong with me. My hair was too short: my mother had cut it into "Sheena Easton," and the feathered sides wilted in the midday heat. Maybe I was paranoid. I hoped the situation would right itself before I went off to the church summer retreat, three days in the redwoods with all the kids from MYF, a chance to be away from parents, smoke cigarettes, and bond with one another. It was *Little Darlings*—and although the thought of losing my virginity was a rather lofty notion for me then, at twelve, it was still in the heady mix of possibilities of being *away at camp*.

I could barely sleep the night before because I was so excited and worried at the same time. I tossed and turned and woke suddenly with the sun shining in my face, not having been aware that I had fallen asleep.

My mother drove me to the church and then inexplicably burst into tears, begging me not to go. I couldn't understand this at all. We had not been getting along lately. None of my family had. My mother and I would fight because I wouldn't practice the piano, my brother and I would fight over the TV, and my father and mother would fight all night long. I pulled away from her as she gained control of her emotions. She was cold again as I left the big yellow station wagon. I was relieved to be getting away from the fighting.

I'd hoped to get a ride with Lotte and Connie, but they'd already gone with Ronny. I was too afraid to ask Carl, the cute monkey-faced popular boy who lived to make me miserable, or Jaclyn and Eugene, the equally simian brother and sister who fancied themselves trendsetters because they'd started hating me long before anyone else.

All the kids had organized themselves into groups riding up together, and since I was late, and hated, I just stood there with my cowboy sleeping bag and tried not to look scared. I reasoned with myself that the more I worried about something bad taking place, the less likely it was to happen. Since I'd been so tortured about this trip, by this law it was bound to turn out fine.

I rode to the camp with the young minister who led the youth group. He never wore a clerical collar and was of indeterminate age—youngish, unmarried, but ageless in the way Korean men sometimes are. As his yellow Pinto puttered up the freeway, I must have fallen asleep because later, close to the camp, I woke up all sweaty.

"You are very cute when you are sleeping." Reverend Soo was always nice to me, in an uncreepy, comforting way. We got to the campsite around the middle of the day. It was hot and teeming with Korean kids. Ronny's fine-ass brother had the door of his Trans Am open, and the stereo was blasting Chicago.

"Everybody needs a little time away, just for the day . . .

From each other . . ."

The beautiful Jolie, who was a few grades above me, perfect in her cut-off jeans and ribbed purple tank, a red bandanna tied suggestively like a garter around her lean thigh, looked over at us and smiled. My heart beat faster. Jolie had never been mean to me, but she'd never spoken to me either. She was way too sophisticated for that. I had a crush on her, but I was too much in awe to even admit it to myself. Whatever Carl or Eugene did to me, it didn't matter unless *she* saw it. If *she* was a witness, then the sting of humiliation would last for days. I think it was less that I wanted her, and more that I wanted to be her. With her taut brown body and baby face, she represented to me the glory of the '80s, the idea that beauty was a powerful thing, that if you looked a certain way, you could have everything.

Around 1985, Jolie turned preppy, and her beauty, her gleam, her youthful sensuality was lost in the translation. But back then, still in her slutty prime, she held all the boys at our church in the palm of her purple-nail-polished hand.

She leaned over to Ronny's brother and whispered something. He grabbed her face and they fell into each other laughing. Oh, to laugh like that, to be held by a boy and get lost in your own wondrous being. To be able to throw your head back like a pony while the boys admired you. To be the object of desire and the one doing the desiring . . . I wished that for myself. As I was lost in this reverie, someone threw a pine cone at my face.

"Oh shit. MORON'S here!!!!"

I tried not to cry as I looked for the perpetrator in the crowd of kids. Jolie stifled a chuckle, biting her tantalizingly glossed lip, and turned her head away. Unable to look at me because it was just too embarrassing, she nuzzled Ronny's brother's golden neck.

The shards of pine cone made my eye blaze red. Half blind, I made it to the girl's cabin without further incident.

The cabins were made of logs. Inside, there were about ten bunk beds, which were exotic and exciting to me, as I'd never slept in one. I looked around for an unclaimed top bunk, but none was to be found. I unrolled my stained old sleeping bag that didn't zip up all the way onto the bottom bunk near the back door.

Jaclyn was in the bathroom complaining to no one in particular, "The food here is so baaaddd!!! I was sticking my finger down my throat trying to throw up. That didn't work so I was on the toilet trying to *crap* it out. I want to go home!"

I wanted to go home, too. This was going to be bad. I could just tell.

Lotte came into the empty cabin and saw me. I was glad to see her and walked up.

"Hi. I just got here. Where is your bunk? I want to be near you guys," I said.

She had a mean smile on her face, but she wouldn't look me in the eye—kind of an "I can't wait to tell my friends this . . ." expression.

She said, "We're over there. It's too crowded already. I'm going to the canoes."

"Well, wait for me, I'm going to change and go down, too."

I ran over to my bunk to get my bathing suit, but she was already gone.

I put on my orange one-piece and an oversize white T-shirt and walked down to the lake.

Carl saw me first.

"Oh shit. It's Moron. Let's drown her. Hey Moron. Why'd you come here? Nobody likes you. It's going to be the worst three days of your life."

"Shut up!" I yelled.

Carl's brother Mike jumped in.

"Don't tell my brother to shut up! You shut up, Moron! MORON!!!!"

I tried to ignore them and got into a boat by myself. Not really knowing how to row, I pushed back from the dock a few feet and panicked. I must have only been about five feet away, but it might as well have been miles because I couldn't move the boat back at all. I was slowly drifting out onto the lake. I envisioned myself washed ashore on a deserted island, far away from the taunts and flying pine cones, meeting Christopher Atkins there in our own *Blue Lagoon*, eating bananas and wearing a loincloth and having sex for the very first time . . .

Carl and Mike started to miss me, I guess, because they started to scream at me.

"MORON! MORON! Just paddle it back. Don't hog the boat, pig! Boat Hog!! MORON!!!"

Lotte, Connie, and Ronny joined them on the dock. They all stared yelling. "MORON!!! God! Can't you do anything? Just paddle it back. We want to go, too. MORON!!! Stupid. C'mon. Hurry!"

I was trying to make the oars move in the water, but they were too heavy. The boat started to drift back toward the dock, but not nearly as quickly as they would have liked, so they all screamed louder.

"MORON! Can't do anything! Why don't you just go home? You are ruining it for everybody. MORON! WE hate YOU!!! MORON!!!! GO HOME! GO HOME GO HOME GO HOME!!!!"

A camp counselor, one of the older Korean girls in Jolie's class, came down to the dock. "Just row it. Just hold the oar. No! Just— come on! Other people want to use the boat, too. Come on. Don't be so selfish. Just row back here. Come on!"

"Yeah, MORON. Do what she says. Come on. MORON! MORON MORON MORON MORON MORON!!!!!!!!!!"

I was not going to cry. I was too old for that. I was not going to give them the satisfaction. My face was red, and my eye still burned from the pine cone. My arms were killing me from rowing. Finally, with a pull on the oars that took all of my strength, the boat banged on the dock.

Carl jumped in the boat and tried to push me in the water, but I was fast and ran back to the girl's cabin.

The cabin was quiet. Everybody was off doing something fun, enjoying the time away from home with friends, getting tan, doing arts and crafts, playing volleyball, going to second base in the bushes. It made the silence unbearable.

I thought I would sleep for a while to make the time go faster. I just wanted to go home. Why did I come? What had I been thinking? That suddenly, when we were all away from home, I would be friends with everyone? But then, it had been only a few weeks ago that I was at Lotte and Connie's house, making plans about coming to the church camp, picking out boys we liked, wishing Connie's sty would go away before the big weekend. Was I losing my mind? What could I have done? Carl and Mike and Jaclyn and Eugene always hated me, but how could they so quickly infect everyone else with that feeling? Hate was contagious, I guess. I was coming down with it, too. I hated myself and sat down on my cowboy sleeping bag.

It made a crunching sound. I looked inside the bag. It was filled with dry leaves, pine cones, sticks and dirt—even dog shit! I heard laughter coming from outside the cabin. I recognized it. It was Lotte and Connie. I couldn't take it anymore and I started to cry. I was a million miles from home, everybody wanted me to leave, and I had just gotten here. Filling up my stained old sleeping bag was so mean, and obviously just the beginning. What else would I have to endure for the next three days?

I went outside to shake out the bag. The girls were gone. I emptied it as well as I could, but it still smelled of eucalyptus and shit. I wanted to wash it, but figured it would be even worse wet. I took it back inside and sat with my head down on the bottom bunk.

Another girl and a boy came into the cabin. A waiflike girl named May Cha stood there with her brother Johnno, a fat kid who had allergies. The area from the bottom of Johnno's nose to the top of his lip was always red and flaking off. He also had dandruff, so when he moved, it was like he was snowing.

May spoke first. "Moron, we don't want you in our cabin. You have to move. We took a vote and everybody voted to have you out."

"Where am I supposed to go?"

"I don't know. Maybe you should go find a big tree and sleep under it. I don't care. You just can't sleep here."

"Did you fill up my sleeping bag with leaves?"

"No. I didn't do that. I just organized the vote to have you kicked out of the cabin. I wouldn't do something like that."

I tried to think of the worst thing I could say. I knew that May wasn't responsible for the bag, but she was a dick all the same. I searched my pre-teen mind for possibilities. "Go climb a rock!" No, too *Yosemite*. "Sit on it." No, too *Happy Days*. Um, um. Ah yes! I have it.

"YOUR MOTHER!!!!!"

"My what?"

"YOUR MOTHER!!!!"

Johnno, who had been silent until then, exploded.

"Take that back, you bitch. What about my mother?!"

In my distress, I had forgotten that they were brother and sister, and in saying something about her mother, I was implicating him as well.

The force of his rage was truly terrifying. He got all flaky on me. It was like an avalanche. His thick glasses steamed up so fast I was sure he couldn't see me at all. It seemed somebody had said "Your mother" to him before, and he just wasn't going to take it anymore.

Johnno lunged at me and grabbed my forearms. I grabbed his in return, and we pushed each other from one side of the cabin to the other. He wasn't very strong, but he was plugged into the same kind of adrenaline that mothers use to lift cars when their children are in peril. I was so surprised that I was fighting a boy that I had trouble getting my footing. He pushed me backward into my still crunchy, cracklin'-leaves sleeping bag, and I dug my nails into his arms and pushed him up against the log wall. It must have looked like we were dancing.

Johnno's nose was running and he was crying hot, angry tears out the sides of his thick glasses. It moistened all the white patches on his upper lip so it looked like he was melting. We were getting tired of pushing each other back and forth.

He let go of my arms, and I let go of his.

"Just get out of here, MORON!"

"Yeah, get out! Get out, MORON!"

"You MORON!!! We don't want you here infecting our cabin. GET OUT GET OUT GET OUT GET OUT!!!!!"

Then, inexplicably, they both left.

I took my sleeping bag to the back of the cabin and shook it out again. Leaves and twigs and dry dog turds and acorns still stuck to the flannel inside and had to be picked out by hand. I would be finding burrs embedded in my skin for days.

As I emptied the bag, I could hear the sounds of summer off in the distance. That Chicago song again, girls screaming, water splashing, intermittent outbursts of the 2-4-6-8 variety—all of it for me was the music of exclusion, the sorry soundtrack of the outcast, reminding me of all the things I was not doing, was not allowed to do, would never be a part of.

The next few days were relatively uneventful. It seems likely a talk was given, the counselors or ministers devising some intervention on my behalf. The name-calling and the shouting and the flying pine cones ceased. All that remained was a sort of silence, a wide berth. Everywhere I went for the next three days, a great deal of space was made around me. It was as if I had an infectious disease. No one would share a table or a bench with me. Not at mealtimes, not at campfires, not at the talent show that I was not allowed to participate in. In the crowded lodge, with kids crammed into every nook and cranny all over the floor, practically hanging from the rafters, I sat with an entire bench to myself. I stayed in the girl's cabin, but all the campers around me had moved their things and were sleeping on exercise mats and chairs pushed together to avoid the five bunks that surrounded mine. I got a top bunk, which I was happy about, but slept with one eye open for three days, fearing attack and ready to fight to the death.

My cootie quarantine was actually more painful than the outright battles. Everybody around me was experiencing the exhilaration of being away from home and around other kids and swinging from ropes and forging friendships that would last a lifetime, while I sat inside, alone in the shadowy cabins, and made God's Eyes out of yarn and chopsticks.

I got home, and my mother was cold and my dad was gone. She never explained where he was; she just stayed in their bedroom with the door shut.

I vowed never to return to that church, and Sunday mornings there would be a near riot with my mother begging, pleading, threatening, denying, bargaining, then finally accepting that I wasn't going with her. There was no way I was going to face those horrible kids again. I'd had enough. I was hated, so I had to hate.

My mother lied about me week after week. I think she went as far as to tell people that I was in boarding school. ("She write me every day!") The abject horror at my refusal to attend church combined with my father's absence made her go insane. She went on a crash diet and got down to 114 pounds and then got a perm to celebrate.

Daddy came home eventually, like he always did, but he was different. He was mean, cold, confusing. He kept a suitcase packed with Gold Toe socks and underwear, ready and waiting at the bottom of the stairs.

May Cha told my mother to tell me that she was sorry about how they had all treated me at camp. She hoped that I would come back someday. She said she wanted to apologize in person. I don't know why, but that embarrassed me tremendously and made me hate the kids even more.

I did agree to go to a church function when I was around seventeen. I wore a flowery dress of my mother's and dyed my hair back to black from the sick pink-orange it had been. My mother was so happy she nearly cried and kept her arm around me the entire time, partly out of love but also to keep me from running away. Lotte and Connie were there, and when they saw me, their faces got red with joy, and I wanted to punch in their hot smiles from the side.

Lotte said, "Oh my God, MORON'S here!" I sat by my parents, seething inside. Went home later. Never let it go.

I went on with the rest of my life. I made some good friends in high school, and it constantly surprised me that I was never betrayed in the same way again. Yet, I didn't let myself get as close to my friends as I would have liked.

My experience with Lotte and Connie taught me to keep people at a distance, and not to worry about what they thought of me. In a sense, it gave me some of the impetus I needed to go out into the world and follow my dreams. It seemed like the worst was over. I could get on with the business of enjoying my life, living it as fully as possible. No matter where I was, I could be happy, since I was no longer stuck at that summer camp, sitting on a log by myself, wishing

I had a pair of cutoffs and some friends. Loneliness became familiar and easy. I played "Chopsticks" alone on the piano, and learned to love every solitary note.

Not too long ago, Ronny came to a show of mine at the Punchline in San Francisco. She came backstage after the show with a group of her friends. She was thrilled to see me and wanted to talk about the days when we had known each other growing up. "Hi—remember me?" I took one look at her and said, "No, I don't. I have no idea who you are." Then I walked away.

My brother remained friendly with Lotte and Connie for years afterward. It makes me feel betrayed that he is close to them, but at least it gives me an opportunity to find out how they are doing. In some way, I suppose I miss them, because I can't seem to let go of their memory. I wish our friendship could have been allowed to grow and change and carry on into adulthood. They were horrible to me, but kids are like that sometimes. I want to forgive and be loving and try to see it from their point of view. My brother says that even now they always ask how I'm doing, and are genuinely happy when he tells them, "She's just fine . . ."

I turned my Korean name, Moran, into one of my most lasting and memorable routines. I portray my mother screaming it through a set of French doors. "MORAN!!!!!!" Why would you name your daughter that? It's like calling your firstborn "Asshill." Now, people call it out to me at shows—"MORAN MORAN MORAN!!!"—and it feels like love.

The cowboy sleeping bag sits in a closet at my parents' house. After 20 years and a lifetime of use, it still smells faintly of sap.

4

POLK STREET

About the time I was recovering from Lotte and Connie's betrayal, my parents sold the snack bar to my uncle and bought a bookstore called Paperback Traffic. It was in the heart of Polk Street, which in the late '70s was the Promised Land for homosexual men from all over the world. I didn't understand it at first. I thought that men and women were together and that was it.

When I called my brother a fag, I didn't know what the word meant. My mother would panic and yell, "That is because she is a lesbian! Now you are even!" Men wanting each other seemed like a mistake. The young boys buying makeup at the Walgreen's on Polk and California were surely buying it for their girlfriends. Weren't they?

Once, walking down the street, I saw a bunch of tough-looking guys dressed in leather chaps and hanging all over the parking meters. I was scared to walk by them because they looked like dangerous criminals, but when I did, they just smiled at me. One of them said, "I like your purse," and pointed to my Hello Kitty bag. I smiled back, swinging the bag in a "Yeah, isn't it great?" fashion, and then I noticed one of them had a pierced nipple! I was so shocked that I could not stop thinking about it for days and days. At school, I would sit at my desk and wonder how he got jewelry there. I thought maybe he had some crazy accident that left him with a hole in his nipple and he decided to be a good sport about it and put a ring in there. Then, I worried and worried that he was going to get it caught on something.

My parents let me run around by myself all the time, and I would walk up and down the street and see those leather-chap guys hiding in doorways and alleys, often one standing against the wall and one kneeling down in front. I thought, "That is so nice. They are fixing each other's zippers."

My mother's explanation of homosexuality was equal parts clear and cryptic. "Sometimes, there is a man and a woman and they like to kiss. But, gay, is man like to kiss the man." I still didn't get it. Were they waiting for the right women to come along? Were they just practicing until they got married? Where were the girls?

I finally got it when I was looking at *Meatmen*, a graphic porno novel that we sold at the store. I stared at page after page of muscled jocks sucking each other off—and I finally got it. These *were* the girls.

When I really understood that I was surrounded by homosexual men, the first thing I felt was *safe*. I felt calm and protected and thrilled at the voyeuristic possibilities all at the same time. I knew I'd be okay. My body had started to develop earlier than other girls my age, and I had been the object of keen interest of many of my father's friends and a male relative, and I had already received countless touches that felt rude and invasive. I was wary of men, especially older ones, and did my best to stay away from their leering glances, grabby hands and personal questions.

Homosexuality brought me back to men, made me see they could be trusted, and even loved. I've never stopped feeling this way.

The men who worked at our bookstore were not like men I had ever seen before. There was Dante, who was thin as a rail, as he was a vegan, another thing I did not understand. He wore huge, dangling earrings on his shaved head, but dressed in just a T-shirt and jeans so it was hard to tell if he was dressed up or down, a woman or a man. I was terrified of him at first, even though his voice was soft as a mouse and he had the shiest smile.

Then, there was Forbes, tall and thin and British, with a sprawling, lavishly detailed Japanese tattoo that covered his entire body. He was funny and bitchy and conservative and sweet all at the same time. Dante, Forbes, and I did not know what to make of each other. They knew nothing of little girls. I didn't get their tattooed arms or earrings.

Oddly enough, my father was the bridge to understanding. "You should talk to them. They know lots about everything. It is so interesting. They are so bright. Forbes is so funny. You will see. Ask them about books."

I didn't want to. I just wanted to read *Dear Abby: The Collected Letters* every day. It embarrassed me, leaving the store with it tucked under my arm, Forbes eyeing it with curiosity. I knew I needed some kind of literary makeover. Dante gave me Heinlein's *Stranger in a Strange Land*. Forbes gave me a French book on autopsy, with the grossest pictures I had ever seen. I was on my way.

John Waters' *Shock Value* came next. I was obsessed with Divine, who I thought was kind of pretty. I had no idea she was a man, even though the book showed her out of drag with a buzz cut and a polo shirt. I thought maybe she was just getting her hair cut short like my aunts did ("So I can just wash and go"). I was looking at the book and I asked Forbes about Divine.

"Well, Petal, first of all. He's a man."

It was like the Birds and the Bees and the Butterflies.

I asked, "Why does he dress as a woman?"

"Because he wants to."

"But why?"

Forbes sighed. "Some do it to be funny. They aren't that cute or whatever, feel somewhat lacking, so they get attention that way. Some just like the way it looks. Some do it because they love women. Some because they hate women. They're all different. It's such a bother really. I couldn't imagine putting all those things on, makeup and binding up your naughty bits. You can see them do shows sometimes. It can be very entertaining. There are clever ones and pretty ones, ones so good you can't even tell they're men and ones so bad you're glad that they are because no woman should have to look like that."

It was becoming so clear—the boys buying makeup at Walgreen's and the overly made-up "women" I would see spilling out of the bars on Polk Street when we'd close the bookstore at night. I would crane my neck out of the back window of my parents' station wagon while we were stopped at a red light, trying to catch a glimpse of the goings-on at Kimo's, the hot nightclub on Pine.

Kimo's was famous for drag beauty pageants like the "Empress of San Francisco," where aging queens would adorn themselves with feathers and false eyelashes and duke it out for the sublime glory of the imperial crown.

The drag queens of my youth were as distant and aloof as the popular girls at my high school. Unattainable and admired, these beacons of femininity taught me about desire from afar. There were two drag queens who worked at the bookstore a few years later. Alan, an anorexic psychology student with horrendous skin, and Jeremy, a tiny blonde who would later gain fame as an artist, painting exquisite objets d'arts entirely out of makeup. They were the main contenders in the Drag Wrestling matches held at the bar called the End Up.

There would be an actual ring in the middle of the club, and the champion, often Alan dressed in a black baby-doll sheer nightie and stiletto heels, would weave her way through the crowd. Her glossy black wig was dark as night and you could tell she had blood in her sights. The spotlight would shine directly on her, throwing her crater-face into relief, and you knew she would win before it even began.

Jeremy would appear from the other side of the club. Teetering on black maribou high-heel mules and wearing a leopard-print pajama set, she had big blonde curls that were all hers, no wig for this tawny beauty. She'd place a pink ribbon high in her hair, and she was as pretty as could be, considering she was about to get her ass kicked.

They didn't shake hands. There was no referee. It just started without warning. Jeremy waved to the crowd and Alan took off a spike heel and knocked her opponent down with it. Negligees were torn off, hair ribbons went flying, narrow limbs snapped through the air and slim bodies bounced off the ropes.

The battle was a dizzying triumph for Alan, who preened on the mat in triumph, clutching a long lock of Jeremy's real hair in her glamour-length Lee Press-On Nails, as Jeremy savored the agony of defeat, lying on a bed of shredded lingerie and fishnet.

These exhibitions were horrific in their ferocity, catfights to the death, biting and scratching and kicking at carefully concealed balls, with the ripping off of the loser's wig as the final act of humiliation. Since Jeremy didn't need a wig, his real hair had to do. Drag queens are capable of great violence. They should be allowed to enter the WWF. RuPaul could take out Stone Cold Steve Austin in a heartbeat with a flutter of one false eyelash. Drag queens are strong because they have so much to fight against: homophobia, sexism, pinkeye.

Jeremy's makeup art was spectacular. He did beautiful paintings, delicate dioramas in nail polish, dreamy watercolors accomplished entirely with Aziza eye shadow. He also did performance art with his drag wrestling opponent.

The last time I saw Jeremy and Alan perform was at the Castro Street Häagen-Dazs. They took over the ice cream counter for impromptu drag queen guerrilla theatre. Jeremy pulled his wiry body on top of the glass counter, then knocked off all the tasting spoons and the cone display. For the grand finale, he shoved a chocolate-dipped vanilla ice cream bar up his ass and then pulled it out and ate it.

Confused patrons who had come in for their after-dinner treat and not for this—the only way to put it—spectacle, fled the premises, and the police were called. By the time they got there, everyone was gone. I wonder who called 911 and cried, "He's shoving ice cream up his ass! Please hurry!"

Jeremy died of AIDS a few years later, but Alan still carried on, studying Melanie Klein and alternately turning tricks as a dominatrix and selling pot from his apartment. He lived in the basement of an old Tenderloin building in an apartment with bloodred walls and the perpetual odor of baby powder, left over from the many bath parties he once had, sensual affairs where guests would fill and refill his claw foot bathtub, washing each other and screwing the night away. We'd smoke his seedy, headachy cheap trannie pot and get high and talk about how much we missed Jeremy.

Forbes and Dante didn't spend much time on Polk Street. They both had boyfriends and led fairly sedate lives, although they did have their draggy moments. One day, a messy brown Jackie O wig appeared behind the cash register, and everyone who worked that day took turns wearing it. First, Dante, who looked like a hip '60s lesbian in it. Then Forbes, who looked like an unhappy secretary. Then me, like a little girl in drag.

Forbes loved black men and Asian men, and he had two boyfriends, Black Gary and Chinese Gary. He also flirted a lot with my father, which I found hilarious. Forbes called him "Joe," the name my father insisted all white people call him. "Oh, Joe," Forbes would often say with a long sigh. "My Joe, those are some snappy pants!" he'd call after my father when he'd wear his ridiculously bright plaid trousers. My father ignored him all the time, just like he ignored me. And Forbes loved it, unlike me.

Forbes, who was also a very talented artist, once presented my father with a portrait done in oil, framed in simple blonde wood. It was so dead-on, the half smile starting in the eyes, the intelligent forehead, the easily annoyed mouth that could go either way. My father seemed uncomfortable with his own image, but he hung it up in our living room anyway.

I'd look at it, marveling at the idea that someone could take your face and put it on a canvas so perfectly, and then have it be more than just your face. That painting was my father so very clearly, the rage and the sweetness all wrapped up in a sweater vest. I hated that painting when I hated him. I loved it when I loved him. My father never mentioned it. It just hung there.

Surprisingly, my father had a history of hating homosexuals. My mother told me the story.

"One time, Daddy have a friend, so close that he is almost, well you know . . . Sometimes when you are young, you have a friend, you love your friend so much you don't know what to do, so with Daddy and his friend, he have this kind of situation. So one day Daddy and his special friend go to a picnic and they drive to the country and they stop car and Daddy's friend say that he love Daddy, something like that. And then he put his hand on Daddy leg, something like that. And Daddy was so shock. And so he punch his friend, and then kick him out of the car and just drive back without his friend. And he never speak to him, see him again. And how much pain is Daddy, because he miss his friend, but Daddy cannot forgive that kind of situation. Because when you young, is not really gay, how they have gay wear the leather pants we see in front of bookstore. Not like that kind of gay. Maybe they become that kind of gay later. When you young, you just love, you don't know what to do. You just love your friend, you don't know what to do."

Years later, after the store closed and all the employees got new jobs and some died and we all lost touch with each other, I came home to attend my grandfather's funeral. My family and I were all bumping around each other in the emotional fog that mourning can bring. My father and I were sitting in the living room, not talking as usual. We were both looking at Forbes' painting, which captured my father in his younger days. We stared at it, quietly and unaware of each other. Suddenly, my father said, "You know, I really loved him."

I felt it. He did love this wild yet oddly conservative homosexual who had tattooed arms and a British accent, a man so unlike himself that the idea of a friendship between them was ridiculous. At that moment, I loved my father more than I ever had. His simple statement made me cry, and I didn't care if he saw me.

5

ON BEING A FAG HAG

I am fortunate enough to have been a fag hag for most of my life. A fag hag is a woman who prefers the company of gay men. The marriage of two derogatory terms, *fag* and *hag*, symbolizing the union of the world's most popular objects of scorn, *homosexual* and *woman*, creates a moniker that most of those who wear it find inoffensive, possibly because it smacks of solidarity.

Some women have come to me urgently expressing their desire for a new name. Countless fruit flies, queen magnets, and even a swish dish or two have begged me to reconsider the title of such an important entity. While no woman wants to be thought of as a "hag," you must acknowledge that the gay man in your life is not concerned with your youth and beauty. He wants to know your soul. He loves you for your courage and intellect. Whether you are lovely or plain, you are beautiful to him for these qualities—and many more.

Similarly, most of the homosexuals I know bristle at the word "fag." It conjures up images of awkward, limp-wristed adolescence, of the taunts and catcalls of bullying jocks who are insecure in their own sexuality, all too willing to lash out to mask their fear.

But when you put these two words together, they seem to cancel each other out. The pain vanishes, and as you know, bees without sting offer only pure honey.

As a teenager, I found myself drawn to the slight, sensitive young men in my theater group, perhaps because they reminded me distantly of my beloved Forbes and Dante. High school was a dangerous place, and my search for sanctuary led me to gay men once again, even if they didn't yet know their own sexual identities. Or maybe they did know and just weren't telling. The only thing that mattered was that we found each other. If you are a gay man, think back on the girl you took to the prom. She was your first fag hag.

I was a loud, fat girl, and saw as my natural companion the fey, lithe boy. We were both scared. Thank God we met.

Growing up, getting older, shedding baby fat for womanly curves, my fag, Berry, watched me burst forth from my fleshy cocoon, and I was suddenly seen by the world as the butterfly he always knew me to be.

I heard his voice get deeper, saw his long limbs become corded with lean muscle. His lips, once hesitant and shy, blossomed sweetly, confident and ready. When we walked down Castro Street together, longing looks would be cast his way, and I saw he was beginning to return them.

We never went home with anyone back in those baby days. We just stayed with each other, watched John Waters' movies late into the night, daydreamed while listening to Roxy Music's *Avalon*, cut each other's bangs, and talked about Madonna and what we'd do when we left school and all the bullshit behind.

Berry cried in my arms after he told his family he was gay, and he let me throw things and break them when I was rejected by my first boyfriend because his friends thought I was too fat.

We sneaked into the gay hustler bars on Polk Street and laughed as the chickens and the chicken hawks cruised each other and ignored us. We dressed each other up and took pictures. When we both got lovers, we weren't jealous. We grew up, but we didn't grow apart.

When Berry was gay-bashed on Market Street, greeting me the next morning with a black eye and a smile on his face, he tried to make the best of it, dismissing the whole thing as "Truly funny, if you really think about it," but I knew that it hurt him more than he could say.

When my parents told me they hated me because I was a failure at everything, Berry baked me a cake, made me a mixed tape, and loved me madly.

Berry and I dressed more and more alike as we got older. We told everyone we were brother and sister, but it is almost as if we were closer than that.

We both tended to pick boyfriends who cared little about us, which makes me glad that we had each other to love.

We are friends even now, in what seems like a lifetime later. We grew together, grew apart, then together again. We still love to make dinner together and talk about the days when everything was new, and life was so exciting because it was just beginning.

If this relationship sounds familiar to you, it is very likely that you are a fag hag. We are from all walks of life, all classes, all ages, all races; straight, lesbian, and somewhere in between. We are as diverse as we are numerous. The common bond that we share is our alliance with gay men, a connection that is both nurturing and powerful, sweet and sour, retail and wholesale.

Although our fag hag experiences vary greatly, there are general-izations that can be made. Fag hags usually make all the plans and see that they are carried out in a manner that pleases both the fag and the hag equally. This is because most of us have a knack at organizing and mobilizing. We are leaders, and keep our troops in line.

Fag hags like to be the center of attention. It is ironic that at a gathering of men, coming together for the sole purpose of meeting one other, they will all spend the better part of their evening hanging on the only woman's every word.

Unfortunately, this situation does not last. By the end of the party, a fag hag often finds herself alone in the room, in the midst of the overflowing ashtrays and half-finished drinks, deserted by all her admirers—who have paired off to admire each other. This brings us to the next fag hag rule of thumb: We always drive ourselves to events, and for the most part, we enjoy going home alone. I suppose it could be looked at as a depressing end to an evening, but I find it joyous. I love to sleep in bed alone, tossing my body in slumber every way I can, waking up without having to kiss some sour mouth or awkwardly realizing I have no idea whom that sour mouth belongs to.

I can carry on with plans I made for brunch without having to consult or bring along the "trick." I don't have to gauge his expression to see whether our drunken episode resulted in a fight and try to gauge his mood. I don't have to dress quietly and duck out the back door, or learn a new language. Tricks are always much more trouble than they are worth. That is why, every Halloween, when I am asked "Trick or Treat," I always err on the side of chocolate. Yes, it's true. I do live in paradise.

Fag hags, contrary to the wisdom of popular culture, are not "beards." The term "beards" refers to the complicit relationships between some women and gay men, wherein they pretend, for the "benefit" of family and sometimes employers, that they are a conventional straight couple. This is so that they might enjoy the "status" of being "normal" heterosexuals.

I find this a violation, a travesty, and an aberration of the fag hag/fag relationship. However, I do not wish to judge those who find themselves in the kind of predicament that requires such a façade. It is not their fault, but the fault of the ignorance of those around them. In my world, honesty rules above all, and the truth helps everyone. So have a beard if you must, but I would prefer that you be clean-shaven.

We fag hags love drama and are skilled thespians on the stage of life. We also crave scandal and gossip. Be warned, we don't keep secrets, we harvest them. Of course, we do know when and where loyalty is required, and in these cases, we are true to our beloved. Bitchiness is always appreciated, and insulting others behind their back is a favorite pastime. This is a way for us to repay the world for the way we are treated. Women and gay men have long been considered second-class citizens by the dominant culture. How do we keep our strength? By talking shit about those who think they can oppress us. Herewith one caveat given me by a particularly elegant and flamboyant gentleman: "Fight fire with *flame!*" Do not underestimate the power of our wagging tongues. Cross us and you will get burned, not licked.

Most of us like to shop and love to be taken to lunch at a restaurant in a department store. Not the food court, mind you. We are still ladies, regardless of how we behave at times.

I still lobby for a "Fag Hag Day," when we might be shown the gratitude we deserve en masse. We are important. We are the backbone of the gay community and as such should be honored! Consider that there are holidays as innocuous as "Secretary's Day"—with special greeting cards to celebrate them. What might a "Fag Hag Day" card look like? Possibly a photograph of a winsome young man in an evening gown, with a darling bit of verse at the bottom:

You have stuck by me now and then,
Even though you know I like men.
We are so close, my sweet fag hag,
Sometimes I think you are me in drag!

Gentle reader, if you wish to join us, I bid you "Welcome" with open arms and an arched eyebrow. Let it be known, however, that this is certainly a profession that chooses you. Many of us did not plan to become fag hags, we just looked around one day and realized that was what we were. Others aspired to greatness, and then greatness materialized around them in the form of a group of cute advertising executives spending Labor Day Weekend on Fire Island.

The fastest way to become a fag hag, if you are so inclined, is to get a job as a makeup artist, but this is not practical or realistic for most. (I do not offer the perfect solutions, only the ones I know work.) Another is to become a grand dame of the stage and screen. For myself, this route has been most rewarding. This way, I can "hag" as many "fags" as I like, and bring to the world this kind of love story that is so common, yet so often overlooked.

Whatever road you take, when you get there, be good to the men in your life and let them take care of you. Know that what you have is precious and holy. Remember, regardless of sexual orientation, men and women will always need each other.

So if you've nothing nice to say, go sit next to the cutest, most elegantly dressed and well-mannered guy at the party. He will appreciate it, I promise.

6

NICKY AND THE NEW SCHOOL

When I was fourteen, I attended a senior party with Jodie Peet. The party was one of those where the parents are out of town and there are a bunch of people passing joints and picking at a turkey carcass. It was in St. Francis Wood, where all the rich kids lived, in a beautiful mansion. The kids' bedrooms all had their own bathrooms, which seemed so extravagant to me, but in one the toilet was broken and there was all kinds of shit floating around in it.

Jodie, a big, tan girl with tiger-colored hair, got seriously drunk almost instantly. I wasn't sure what to do with her, because I was supposed to be spending the night at her house. I kept trying to get her to stand up, but each time she'd roll back to the ground, getting her khaki shorts all dusty from the gravel in the garden. She'd laugh and say, "You know, we are really good friends. I love you Margaret . . ." and then start laughing and falling down again. At first, I thought she was faking it, but I couldn't get her to move, so I guessed she was really fucked up.

This guy named Nicky who was twenty-two and had a hot senior girlfriend named Jennifer, with big, blonde hair and who looked like she was thirty-six, offered us a ride. It was nonspecific. There was no predetermined destination. He just said, "Ride." I should have known then what would happen. I should have told him to take us home. I should have told him we were going to her house. I should have never been born.

I remember the thrill of being in this car with a MAN and how strange it was. He was flirting with me and he said, "I'm so lucky, to have such a cute girl in the car. I better watch myself!" I was so nervous that I was acting like he wasn't talking to me, so he just kind of stopped.

Jodie was passed out in the back as we drove up to his apartment on Oak Street, a few blocks up from my uncle's snack bar in the bowling alley. I didn't say anything. I tried to think of it as an adventure. I was not going home, and nobody would know. I was not in trouble. I could spend the night here and go home the next day and not be in trouble. I could spend the night at a man's house and not be in trouble.

We walked up to his top apartment, and he carried Jodie into his roommate's bedroom while I waited for him in the hallway for a second. He came out, led me into his bedroom, and then he went back down the hall. I sat down on his bed. I was tired but still amazed that I was in this guy's apartment. I lay down on the bed and waited. I wondered if I was just gonna stay like that all night. I could hear him moving around in the hallway, but no lights were on.

Pretty soon, he came into his room and sat on the bed. He started touching me, and I felt so weird. I wanted to say, "What about Jennifer?" and "We can't do this to her . . ." because that is what it seems that adults say to each other, but I couldn't talk. I was in shock because I didn't know him. He was on top of me and it happened so quickly. I didn't say yes, but I didn't say no either. It was like a flash and he was inside me and it felt cold and hurt in a way that I couldn't explain and I thought: He is raping me, yes, he is raping me—or is he? I did not say yes, but I did not say no. During it, I silently thanked my family for making me go to long church services, because that taught me to leave my body at a young age—those skills really do come in handy, you end up using them in life, not like algebra. Then, he was done, I guess, because suddenly he gave a great sigh, and between my legs it was wet and slimy and it smelled like bleach. He got off me and fell next to me and said nothing. Within seconds, his breathing got heavy and he started to snore.

I got up and walked around the bachelor apartment in the dark. The kitchen was furnished with dirty dishes piled precariously on top of each other. I wanted a cigarette. I wanted to lie in bed with Nicky and smoke with the sheets tucked underneath my arms and tell him it was good for me. I wasn't a virgin anymore. I wanted to tell him, but I don't think he would have cared. I wanted to cry, too, which was confusing, because I was supposed to have been glad that this older guy with a hot senior girlfriend and I had had sex. We had sex. I have had sex. Is this sex? Yes, I have had it. It did not feel good. It hurt a lot. But I have done it.

I went back to the bedroom and wedged myself next to Nicky and stayed awake until the sun came up. Nicky got up, didn't say anything. He looked sick, not as cute. He turned away from me and got out of bed. I sat up and waited. He came in and asked, "Can I give you guys a ride somewhere? I gotta get going." He didn't look at me when he said it. He didn't look at me at all.

Nicky dropped Jodie and me off around Ninth and Judah, and we went to the Raintree Café and ate toast with marmalade. I really hate marmalade. It's bitter. You shouldn't do that to oranges. Not only that, there's rind in it. I told her about what happened with a secretive hush and maybe a little bit of pride—I am not sure why I was proud, it was actually so terrible, but that seemed to be the best way to react to the situation.

We didn't call it rape back then. To us, rape was what happened to hitchhikers and to single women living in ground-floor apartments by men in ski masks. Rapists were not guys we knew who dated the popular girls at our school. We thought what happened was passion, romance, ravishment. It felt wrong to me, but I still defined it in those terms because those were all we had.

At school, Jodie told everyone what had happened.

This redhead named Don, who I had such a crush on, teased me about Nicky relentlessly. I don't understand why, maybe he was jealous. It made me feel like dying. He didn't know what really happened, but it hurt to hear him talk about it like I had enjoyed myself. "You're just pining away for that Nicky boy! Well, I wouldn't hold your breath. I doubt that guy is going to call you. . . . You're just heartbroken. Hey, at least you got some! Probably the last time you ever will."

Years later, this same Don came to a show of mine and sat in the front row proudly, as if to say, "I knew her when." I completely ignored him. They always come back, don't they—like boomerangs and bad chili.

When I taped my first TV appearance for MTV's *Half-Hour Comedy Hour* in 1990, I made a grand and stunning debut. That night, I was hailed as the new star of the San Francisco scene. Everything was bright with lights and hope for the future. I walked around with a scarf wrapped around my head and they said I was like the "Comedy Madonna," which was the best thing you could call me, even now.

Then, I saw him. Nicky was staggering around the back of the theater. He looked at me and stopped and said, "Hey—you were really grea . . ." He trailed off, as I presume he had an awful moment of recognition. He knew who I was and it seemed like the shame of me knowing and him knowing took him over for a second. In the sickening silence, I walked past him without acknowledging him. And still to this day I drive by that shitty apartment on Oak Street and I look up into the broken windows and there is part of me still up there in that place.

At fifteen, I was expelled from my high school for having a 0.6 GPA (all F's and an Incomplete). I'd been attending Lowell, a "special" school for kids with above-average intelligence, and there was little space in the classes for deadbeats like me. I preferred spending my days cutting with the bad kids, drinking and smoking pot, kicking back in unoccupied houses while their parents were at work. I liked it even more than my classmates, and I never rotated out of the "Cutting Club" to catch up on homework and missed tests. I just let myself flunk out. It actually required some effort on my part to accomplish this. I achieved entire semesters of nonattendance, while still keeping up this elaborate day-in-day-out-riding-the-bus-with-a-backpack scholastic ruse. Eventually it caught up with me, and I was expelled, which was totally unacceptable for a nice Korean girl like myself. My parents were so ashamed that they practically disowned me. My entire life, they put so much importance on education, always telling me that they had sacrificed their lives so that I could go to a good school, and here I was throwing it all away.

They had a right to be angry, I suppose, but their views were pretty extreme. Another Korean kid who went to my school stabbed somebody at the 7-Eleven and went to prison. My father defended him saying, "At least he had good grades." What is that? I guess there's lots of time to study in jail.

I guess I was lucky that I disappointed my parents so young that they didn't expect anything from me after that. It was a kind of freedom that really propelled me into the life I have now. I didn't have to impress anyone. I didn't have to go to a good school. I had nothing left to do but pursue my dreams. In a sense, I had nowhere else to go.

The dean let me finish the semester and then I had the summer to decide what to do next.

Getting expelled from Lowell was certainly a blessing, although it didn't feel like it at the time. Underneath all the feelings of failure, I was secretly relieved. I didn't fit into the scene there. Katherine, my former best friend, told everyone I was a lesbian, and when I got upset about it, the girls smoking cloves in the "Pit" told me my reaction was proof that I was indeed a homosexual. The boys made me feel invisible, and the girls were mean and shallow. Cutting class and buying 151 Bacardi and squatting at someone's house while their parents were at work was getting old. It was time for a change.

The summer after I was expelled, the university near my house offered a summer stock theater program for high school kids. It offered college credit, which satisfied my parents, who were shell-shocked from my scholastic demise. Don, the horrible redhead preppy boy who I had an inexplicable crush on, berated me for my decision.

"Why would you want to get college credit now? College is supposed to be the best time of your life. You want it to last forever." That comment stung, as secretly I knew that I would never really go to college, that my grades were so terrible that I would never go past a JC. The university doors would remain forever closed to me, except for here, in the theater department, where there were no embarrassing inquiries about grades or test scores.

Performing, which was such a secret wish, the truest desire of my heart, was what I was forced to choose when the dreams of my parents were turning into nightmares. In the beginning, I disappointed everyone, except myself. The theater department at San Francisco State smelled of industrial-strength cleanser and cigarette smoke. The scent made me feel giddy and free, like a woman in the making.

At first, I was not well liked in the company. I started a week later than everyone else because of some scheduling error, and because I didn't feel welcomed by the suburban rich kid baby fags and drama queen fat girls, I skipped quite a few days on my own. I was not the biggest outcast, however. A guy named Rudy, who had twisted one of his testicles in a fantastic masturbation accident, held that distinction.

I befriended a young punk rock girl named Claudia, who had a

BASH (Bay Area Skin Head) girl haircut, slightly reminiscent of a Franciscan monk, and we sat on the grass in the quad and talked about Siouxie and the Banshees.

A beautiful girl named Lauren with red Madeline Kahn hair and a penchant for calling people who annoyed her "clits" was the informal leader of the pack. She mesmerized me with her ivory skin and stick-like arms and legs. Lauren would lean her enormous carrot-topped head back and swoon like a girl in a Maxfield Parrish painting, and in her I found an entirely different kind of role model. The girls I had crushes on before Lauren were conventionally pretty and had the kind of power over men that I hoped one day I would wield. But Lauren had power over women too. Not only that, Lauren had power, purely in and of herself. It was like she didn't need anyone, she seemed entirely self-sufficient, which wasn't exactly true. She did need an audience.

We sat before her in rapture as she disclosed various secrets to us.

"I was in trouble, because I eat too much fruit and vegetable and not enough meat."

"Last summer, the first time I had done the program, I stayed in the dorms. One night, a jealous and mean fat girl came into my room, and cut off my tail. I had this long, red tail that I had been growing for years. It went down the middle of my back. I woke up and it was next to my head on the pillow. I felt castrated."

"I swing both ways. Yes, I am bisexual. I love men *and* women."

Lauren took a special interest in Piero, a handsome Italian boy from Union City, who never spoke except to say that the ballerina girls who stayed in the dorms next to the theater girls were so young that it hurt to fuck them because they were too tight. He also told me that I should lose weight.

Lauren would straddle Piero on the hallway couches where we'd smoke during the break, and give him a hard-on that he would have to walk off outside before coming back into the Set Design class. I imagined losing tons of weight and coming back the next year, thin and hopefully white, to straddle Piero just like my heroine had done.

Fifteen years later, I was walking down dirty, crowded Nieu Voorburgwal in Amsterdam, and I heard a small voice call my name. It was Lauren. She was older, shier, still beautiful, but changed.

"When I was back in the States last year, I saw your picture on the cover of a magazine. I couldn't believe it. You've done so well for yourself. Congratulations."

She was so timid, so reserved. I wonder what had happened to make her that way. All the force of her being, all the titian red hair and passion, the art nouveau curves of her body, the careless decadence of her sexuality, everything had disappeared. She looked the same, but what I had come to think of as "her" was missing. We met for drinks that night on a floating bar on one of the canals. She brought her shy Dutch boyfriend, who loved Nico and silence. He seemed to tone down the now colorless Lauren even more. I felt hostile, getting drunk when I wanted to get stoned, being eaten alive by mosquitoes, being let down at every turn by my teenage role model, who had grown up disappointingly, living in a foreign country, getting bored among the boring.

Later, we ditched her boyfriend and perused the sex shops that lined the Red Light District. We discussed spanking and the importance of a steady hand and true conviction in a proper disciplinarian. We laughed a lot, and I saw the old Lauren come back, briefly, like a hot flash. Like lightning, but without the delayed assurance of thunder. Lauren had lost her thunder. I think I might have stolen it. It was unfair of me to think it was her fault. I just loved her so much from where I was standing. I took what she was and ran away, to reinvent myself in her image.

Years before, after the last party of the season, we all had stayed up at a professor's house, not wanting the summer or our youth to end.

Lauren held my hand as I made everyone cry with a manipulative speech about how I knew no one had liked me at the beginning of the program. We pledged that whenever we heard the song "This Must Be the Place" by the Talking Heads, we would think of that summer, when we were still young enough to dream of all that might be, and wise enough to know that we wouldn't all make it. That night, Durant, a boxy, shorthaired fag-in-progress, refused to kiss me, even when I insisted that he do so, and he left without saying good-bye.

Claudia and I remained close and I visited her at the spare Redwood City apartment that she shared with her mother. Her mom had gone to England for the remainder of the summer, so I crashed there with Claudia and her best friend, Trace. It was a wonderful two weeks of tarot card reading, female bonding, past life regression, vegetarian cooking, Siouxie and the Banshees analyzing, and goddess worshiping. I'd never felt closer to anyone. I felt loved and accepted, just as myself. We laughed a lot. We didn't even need drugs then. In fact, I don't think we drank or did anything more potent than smoking Camel filters and talking about what we would do to Jim Morrison if he were still alive.

I felt safe with those girls. There was nothing that we couldn't do, or talk about, or imagine together. I felt like I had friends who liked me for who I was, and I felt confident for the first time in my life. I found the courage to move on, to the new semester in a new school and to a new life.

At the very last moment, I had an opportunity to audition for the School of the Arts. I originally had planned to attend Lincoln, the high school in my district, where I assumed I would spend my time in the hallways dogging people until I got stabbed. My blonde Communist friend, Alexi, another girl from the summer stock, went to SOTA, and suggested that I prepare a monologue and try my luck. I did a piece from Elizabeth Swados' *Runaways*, and found a place in the Class of '87.

Since I had a couple of friends at the school already, it wasn't that scary to start over. Seeing the dancers walk around campus with their turned out feet and tights, it felt like I was in *Fame*.

We spent most of our days in movement and acting workshops, and then took the few required courses like math and English in the afternoon. I made friends quickly in the drama department, something I'd never really done before. I felt comfortable with all the freaks, the stoner girls and the fags-in-progress. I joined an improv group called Batwing Lubricant, and we scandalized the whole school with our sketches about the mean janitors. Being in front of an audience was a natural, easy thing. For the first time in my life, I knew exactly what I was doing.

7

DUNCAN AND BOB

With the friends I made at SOTA, the friends I had made at summer stock and the new laissez-faire attitude of my parents ("She couldn't possibly do anything worse"), my social calendar started to heat up. I was feeling more and more like an adult every day, yet without any responsibilities. I loved my new school and kept up my grades there to stay eligible for the theater program.

Claudia had moved to England, and Trace and I started to hang out together in San Francisco. We went to Berkeley, going to huge parties at Barrington Hall, the run-down hippie residence on campus, the center of drug-trafficking and political activity. I assembled an odd collection of friends: Claudia's brother Martin; AJ, an artsy dreamer boy from the summer stock program; Katya, a tall blonde hippie dream girl; Trace; and me, wearing all Trace's tie-dyed skirts and scarves. And there was Duncan.

"Average is stupid," he said. "Understand that and life becomes much easier for us."

Duncan said "us" and it was special. That meant I counted among those he considered above average and it felt good to me. He was so skinny and so blonde, though he always wanted to be slate-gray, like some old woman. He finally found the perfect shade in the washed-out

53

state of Manic Panic's Purple Haze. We met at Barrington Hall in a haze of drugs and pot smoke. Over fettuccine with Grape-Nuts sprinkled on top, we talked like '60s revolutionaries. It was Berkeley in the '80s, which was a sad echo of past glory, but I reveled in his indoctrinating me with his ideology of superiority. I made him laugh when I said Jerry Garcia should launch his own line of skin-care and beauty products, and that with every $12.50 purchase of fragrances, you would get a free bong.

Staying up all night then was still such a thrill. Duncan was a drifter and a visionary, even though he could never really hold down a job or an apartment for very long. We all followed him with a devotion that was part worship, part codependence, part love, and part wonder that he could get away with it. He was older than me, and wiser by far. I realized the guys that I had known before were so fucked. Here was someone who was infinitely cooler than all of them and he wanted to be friends with me, simply because he liked to hear me talk. He was a walking miracle. We went along the same path for years, doing drugs with that same crowd, every day, and drinking whatever we could get our hands on. We took many spiritual journeys, all with Duncan as leader.

He preached the virtues of homemade beer, the cover of "Soul Kitchen" by X, and the sublime combination of coffee and pot. We eventually met his sister and brother, the beautiful Charity and the too-intelligent-to-be-sane Sean; and they were at once familiar and enigmatic, just like Duncan.

Duncan and I were never romantically involved, but we talked about having kids someday. We wanted a son, whom we would name Mordred. He'd have my black hair and Duncan's blue eyes, his father's wisdom of the ages and my love of punk rock.

Things started to change after a while. You can't think drugs are going to keep their magic. Pretty soon, you sense that they are just chemicals, and the people around you are just as fucking lost as you are. After a few months of doing drugs casually with friends, I was on my way to a bad habit. I was only sixteen, but I felt old, and I needed crystal to keep the world sparkling.

I called up Duncan in Berkeley one night and begged him to come into San Francisco and score some speed. He heard an urgency in my voice that frightened him. He wouldn't do it. Because he didn't, I realize now that he probably saved my life. He made me see that my hobby was turning into a full-fledged jones. I was mad at him then, but not anymore.

I was mad at Duncan again when he died. Guys like that are never supposed to die. They are supposed to stick it out to the bitter end, the last ones to leave the party.

Even though we had been out of touch for years, and were not on the best terms when we had drifted apart, the pain of his death struck me like a wrecking ball. I walked around flattened with grief. I missed the funeral because I had a gig and couldn't get out of it in time. I regret that. I know he would have wanted me there.

For months, I dreamed of the long, blonde hair on his arms brushing against me, and when I woke up in the middle of the night, I could smell him. In my dreams, we still talk every so often, on a bad connection to the other side. He always says, "Wish you were here . . ."

Duncan had many different and unusual living situations: houseboats, squats, group houses. He always had a selection of interesting roommates who became a dating pool for me and my friends.

That's how I met Bob, who was twenty-six. I was sixteen. Bob and I went out for almost a year. I can't understand why I always had such bad taste in men. Maybe I valued myself so little that I felt any guy who was interested in me had to be my boyfriend, because beggars can't be choosers or something ridiculous like that.

First of all, Bob was really short, about four inches shorter than me, and I'm not that tall. He also had a monkey body, really long arms and short legs. He was already balding and had a very small ass. He looked like a conservative insurance-salesman type, but not ugly. It was more like if Robert Redford was in a weird scientific experiment and accidentally started de-evolving, and then took the antidote that stopped him halfway to becoming an ape. In fact, that is exactly what he looked like.

Bob lived with Duncan and some hippies and anarchists in a communal house in Berkeley. He wore tie-dyed shirts and listened to bootleg tapes of Greatful Dead concerts for hours on end, but he was as uptight as could be. We'd smoke pot in his tiny Honda Civic, and the entire time he would be looking around, telling us to hurry, always saying, "Are you guys done? Jesus! Is that the cops?" After every hit he would go, "Okaaayyyy," and start the car, like it was time to pack up and move on.

He wanted to be a hippie, but so much of the time he acted like an old man. I hated him the first time I spoke to him, but that didn't stop me from practically moving into his apartment after the first date.

The first night he took me to a Japanese restaurant, and we ate tempura and udon and talked about Tina Turner. "She's a deeply sexy woman," he said. I did not disagree, but it made me uncomfortable right away. What did "deeply sexy" mean? Maybe it is something adults say. Maybe I was too young to understand. His apartment had just burned down, so I suggested that we go to the burned-out shell of the place and look around. I didn't feel like talking to him anymore, so I thought if we went somewhere private, we'd just have sex and then I could go home. The keys still worked, even though the door was scorched black. The smell was unbelievable, charred wood and a sweet, mysterious, burned plastic under-stink. There was no electricity and we walked around using a lighter that would get too hot to use. In the dark, we managed to find the bed and got it on fast and furiously. It surprised me how little I felt when he touched me.

My ex-boyfriend had excited me so much that I would almost faint whenever he did the slightest thing. Bob farted and then came. I cleaned up a little, using the toilet in the dark, and said I needed to go home. I wanted to get out of there. Not having anything else to say, no more sex to have, surrounded by the fire smell and the dripping water, it felt like the end of the world. I noticed later that every building Bob lived in seemed to burn down. I guess it was all the crackheads around Lake Merritt, where he would rent those crappy apartments. Or maybe he was made of flint.

With the exception of the first night, I found that Bob was impotent as well as paranoid, but I wanted to get out of my parents' house and Bob had an apartment in Oakland, so it was perfect. I would get depressed sitting in his apartment waiting for him to get off work at Shenanigan's, so I'd smoke pot and go to the Chinese market and look at weird turtles and eat litchi nuts and sleep for hours in the middle of the day. I felt like an old woman, even though I was a kid.

I stayed in that apartment, stuck with Bob, until he decided that to get over his impotence problem, he needed to have sex with me and Trace at the same time. We had done tons of Ecstasy and the three of us were lying on Bob's futon, tripping out of our minds. My eyes were not focusing properly, so everything in the room was blurry. The drugs were making my eyeballs shake, which wasn't totally unpleasant, just hard to see. I focused on the blob next to me, and I realized that Bob and Trace were making out! I was alarmed, but so high I didn't know what to do. I was kind of strangely flattered that my friend wanted to kiss my boyfriend. That made me like him more.

We went to sleep, but Bob never let it go. He kept talking "three-way! three-way! three-way!" like there was no tomorrow. It was just like that Albert Brooks sketch, where he has two female roommates and he keeps trying to get it on with them. Trace got freaked out. "Oh my God. No offense, but your boyfriend is totally gross. I am not having sex with him. I would do you in a second, but him—no way!" We laughed a lot about it, but inside, it hurt me to be in a relationship with someone so sleazy, and not only that, my best friend knew it.

"It's my fantasy. I've always wanted to have sex with two girls at once. It's my fantasy. It's my fantasy." He kept on, like I needed to hear that because it was his fantasy, I had to do something about it. "But I think that if we did it babe, babe, please, just one time, then I would be over the whole impotence thing. Please babe. Please. It's my fantasy."

His impotence *was* really annoying. I'd have to rub his dick, rub it and rub it so hard I thought that a genie was going to come out and grant me three wishes. The first one would have been "Get rid of this guy!" After rubbing it, it would get semi-hard and then I would have to shove it in me as fast as I could, so he wouldn't lose his erection. There wasn't time for a condom, forget that, because if I hesitated, even for a moment, it would go from semi-hard to semi-soft, and then downright spreadable. I would be reduced to trying to stuff it in me like a magician's handkerchief.

There wasn't that much to put in. Bob's penis was infinitesimal, the smallest one I had ever seen. That doesn't mean anything in general, I believe. The hottest guy I have ever been with was not terribly well endowed, but that never stopped him from satisfying me every time. It's not the size of the penis, it is the size of the spirit and the size of the love that matters.

Bob was such an exercise in lack, his dick was practically an "innie." I knew so little about men and sex and myself, and had been brought up with so few expectations from life, that lack felt comfortable and familiar.

Bob would try to move his baby thing back and forth inside me until it got hard again, with his tongue stuck out slightly and his forehead beaded with sweat and concentration. If we were very lucky, he would ejaculate thinly, leaving a tingly little pool of sticky whiteness that would harden on the polyester sheets. Usually, he would get frustrated in the middle of the pumping, and pull his softie out of me and pout. I'd have to spend the rest of the time comforting him, assuring him of his manhood, letting him know it was okay, that it didn't matter, that I just liked being with him anyway. I gave him hugs and pep talks until I was blue in the face, and told him that worrying about it would cause only more stress. Bob had a problem with stress, and his hair fell out in handfuls because of it.

Our entire sex life became a project directed to and for the achievement of HIS ORGASM, which was the most important thing in the universe. I was so glad when he got off, that I would almost come with relief, but of course, I never did, and of course he never even tried. I think that is what makes me the most angry in retrospect. He never even tried. Not once. He lived in a world where everyone looked out for himself, and I desperately wanted to leave that planet.

He had borrowed $300 from me early in the relationship, and I wanted to get it back before I broke up with him, because I was afraid of never seeing that money again. It was a lot for me at the time, since I was still living with my parents. That money represented saved allowances dating back to 1979.

He kept insisting on the three-way, though, and one night I just had enough. When he was out working his shift at Shenanigan's, Trace came over to his apartment and we packed all my stuff in boxes and ran into the night, laughing our asses off the entire time, thinking about his hair falling out the moment he realized that I had left him.

I went to my parents' house, and he called me in shock.

"Baby. Why, why are you doing this to us? I thought things were so good between us. What is it?"

"I don't know what to say. I am sorry."

Hearing his tiny, hurt voice over the phone made me instantly regret everything. I was scared that I would never make another man as sad again, and knowing that I had that power over Bob made me want to stay with him.

But as I was considering it, he got all mad and hung up on me. I started to laugh and cry at the same time. He was so ridiculous and dramatic, but it was exhilarating because it was being directed at me. I had never felt that I was the object of anyone's desire, much less passionate rage. It was powerful and scary. The phone rang again and I picked it up. It was silent on the other end.

"Hello? Hello?"

No sound, or maybe just hair falling on the floor.

"Hello? Bob?"

"Who do you think it is, bitch?"

He hung up again.

This went on for quite a long time. He finally got tired of calling and hanging up, but I insisted on getting my money back from him, so we arranged to meet the following week, once things had cooled down a bit.

We met at the Chattanooga Café, a run-down old coffee house on Haight Street. Bob was late, and I was anxious. Finally, he walked in wearing a tie-dyed T-shirt and a brand new bald spot. I felt sorry for him, and knew that if I just said that I wanted him back, it would make everything so much more pleasant, but I didn't want to do that, no matter how uncomfortable I was.

I always want to please people. I hate it when someone is mad at me. It is so frightening. I will bend over backward to make sure everything is okay. That is probably why I stayed in this relationship so long, because I knew that he'd be angry if I tried to leave. I never did learn my lesson. I've stayed this way my entire life. At least now I pay more attention to my own happiness, and try to remember that it comes first.

Bob smiled and said, "I'm not proud of my behavior."

I was so relieved. He was apologizing to me!

"Oh, Bob, it's okay. You had a right to be angry. I mean, it was all me. I am so sorry."

"Oh, Baby, that is like sweet music to my ears. You don't know how hard this has been. I miss you so bad."

"I, I . . ." I didn't miss him. I didn't miss him. I was so happy without him . . . but I said it anyway.

"I miss you really bad, too."

His face lit up even more.

"So when are you gonna come back? I mean, you don't have to move back in right away. Maybe we should take it slow. Just see each other a few nights a week. Get to know each other again. It's so wonderful. I knew that you wouldn't let me down. I . . ."

"No. I can't. I thought you understood. I'm not coming back. I don't—I don't want this. I don't want this. I am so, so sorry. I never meant to hurt you, Bob. I just . . ."

He got sweaty looking at me. He was so mad I could see him getting red.

"Bob. Bob. Are you okay?"

After a small period of sweat and silence, he pulled out a wad of bills from his pocket. "That's $300. You can count it if you don't trust me."

"Of course I trust you. Do you want something to drink?"

I searched for something to say to comfort him. I tried being playful.

"Why don't you buy me a milk shake?"

He exploded.

"WHY DON'T YOU BUY ONE YOURSELF! YOU ARE LOADED!!!!"

I tried to stay calm, like it was totally normal for this prematurely middle-aged man to be screaming at me in the cafe. I got up and ordered a chocolate milk shake at the counter and brought it back to the table. My head was spinning with joy, as I felt the roll of bills in my pocket, hard and substantial. It felt like freedom, or at least the cash to buy it. I sipped the cold, creamy melted ice cream and held my breath.

Nobody said anything. Not for a long time.

Then suddenly, Bob got up and said, "FUCK YOU AND EVERY-ONE WHO LOOKS LIKE YOU!!!!!!!!"

He ran out of the café. I started to laugh and laugh, out of a sense of relief and gratitude and out of a strange sort of pride. I had, for once, stood up for myself and stuck to what I knew was best for me, even though I wanted to please Bob and not be the bad guy. I did not stop laughing for a long time. I couldn't believe that Bob, who was a decade older than me, was so incredibly immature. I felt strong, self-reliant and capable. At sixteen, I felt well on my way to becoming a woman.

Some time later, my friends and I were having coffee on Telegraph Avenue and I saw Bob walk down the street with a hippie girl. He was wearing the same tie-dyed shirt and some shorts that showed the crack of his extra-small ass. I screamed and hid behind my friends. He didn't see me, thank God, as he was lost in his girlfriend, who had put her hand on his ass (covering the whole ass), and walked away into the heart of Berkeley.

Years later, I worked in Tempe and one of the waitresses asked me if I knew a man named Bob _____. The name made my blood run cold. I hadn't heard it in years. She said he was the creepy manager of the apartment building she lived in back in Oakland and he'd get the young tenants high and hang around for uncomfortably long periods of time. She told me that once when they were all stoned and watching Comedy Central, I came on and he got all misty and reminisced about how he and I used to be together. That is pretty lame for someone whose last words to me were: "Fuck you and everyone who looks like you."

8

STAND-UP AND SM

With Bob out of the way, I could completely focus my energy on being a drug addict.

Pot had been a cure-all for me for most of my life. When I lived in my parents' moldy basement, I smoked and smoked to forget my life. When I was on the road, I smoked to forget where I was. When I was at home, I smoked to celebrate. It almost didn't affect me anymore. My head would get a little hazy and warm and my throat would get dry and I would be immediately self-conscious or hungry. For some reason, I equated this feeling with peace.

Pot is an insidious drug because it can steal your life away from you, without you even being aware of it. I had a love affair with pot for ten years. Pot was my most devoted partner.

I was fifteen when I met pot—back on an old railroad track behind my high school with two guys named Chris Long and Ken Datre. Ken called me "Baby," which is astounding to a fat teenage girl, who feels invisible and sexless. We smoked a badly rolled, spittle-wet, seedy, paraquat-laced joint. It made me feel tired and as heavy on the inside as I was on the outside. I went home and crashed for hours.

Pot got me deep inside my head to a safe place. I wanted to go back there all the time. I lived there for a decade. It got me to sleep, which I could never do with my parents fighting and screaming at each other all night. It helped me eat, drowning out the existential pain even further with entire boxes of macaroni and cheese, deli potato salad, potato chips and cereal. It was just the state I needed to live in at the time.

When things got really depressing, I'd wake up at two in the afternoon, so far into my head that I'd almost turned inside out. I was living back at my parents' house after the brief stab at "independence" at Bob's. Being sixteen isn't easy for anyone, but I had to make it harder for myself by being expelled from school, having a horrible twenty-six-year old boyfriend, and a quickly escalating drug problem. I couldn't take the nights alone without blowing pot smoke out the window of the basement bedroom. The carpet looked like a pizza, and I would have killed myself without the pot and *SCTV* reruns on Nick at Nite. I stayed an addict out of fear, fear that this was my life, and that I couldn't escape without stoner-sleepwalking my way through it.

As much as I loved being high, I also loved copping. Paging the dealer and the beautiful sound of the ring of him calling you back. Then, nervously going to pick up the drugs, the entire time envisioning

DEA agents kicking in the front door as the money changed hands. I loved the fast exchange and hasty exit, escaping the dealer's house with a huge beautiful green bag of perfect weed—once I got one that looked just like Easter grass—sticky and voluminous. It would always fill me with hope and renewal and good will toward man. I got out of buying drugs what most people got out of Christmas. It also made me feel like I knew how to take care of myself, and that even though the world was a scary, unsure place, everything would eventually turn out okay.

I copped from a friend at work, who got it from some artsy old man who lived on the beach and who got high and stared at the water all day. What a beautiful life!

Oh! The drug dealers I have known. One guy sold dime bags out of his mail slot, conveniently located behind Petrini's Market on Masonic (where a friend got stabbed in the meat department). You'd step down into the doorway and tap on the door, and fingers would take your ten and hand over a little plastic packet of verdant dreams, and that was that. No conversation, no feigned friendship in the uneven power play between addict and pusher. You didn't have to talk about bands you didn't like, or even break open the bag and smoke the token joint with the dealer. Best of all, there was no painful waiting for the phone to ring after you had paged your dealer—watching the minutes ache by as your jones got stronger and threatened to take you over. Even though the waiting could be unbearable, you could console yourself with the thought that any second, he might call, any second your whole day could change, and that made the ache perversely fun. This place was like a drug drive-through, and acquisition met desire in a perfect dance. Walking home from work, I could duck in that doorway, and within the space of a minute, I felt complete. In those days, I found true happiness in my empty house, midday rain outside and a new stash in. You almost didn't have to get high—just knowing that you were going to momentarily, and then later, and again and again. I darkened that drug doorway many times—I even got inside once or twice. The guy that ran the place looked just like Santa Claus. He started selling bad, powdery, baby laxative crank out of the mail slot and the whole operation soon ended. I miss him to this day. He showed me that life as an addict could be surprisingly easy. A mail slot and ten dollars and a little bag of green could bring such happiness. That was the best way to get drugs.

The worst way was hanging out with Cone. Cone was this disgusting guy who was friends with my friend June's dad. He sold drugs to us—but we had to spend a long time talking to him, because he wasn't even exactly a dealer. He was some kind of a middleman, a pusher once removed. We spent days waiting around for other dealers, hanging out at his scary house. Cone hung carpet over the door of his bedroom so that it was soundproof. This was doubly evil because not only could nobody hear you scream, but the fabric would soak up the smells of pot, gross pot dealer guy BO, and the faint sour-ball smell so specific to Cone, and recirculate it around the room. There was a whole lotta foul going on. Cone was fat, but he wore these tight Daisy Duke shorts that not only went up his ass but up in the front, too, so it looked like he had a vagina. One time, I accidentally took his turquoise-and-silver-covered Bic lighter and he came over to my apartment to get it back. My roommates and I clung to the walls so he couldn't see us in the windows, and screamed silent screams, sneaking looks outside to see the side view of his Man-gina as he banged against our front door. Cone had a big-screen TV and always stopped at the Playboy channel and lingered over the soft-core porn until we would yell at him to change it. As we waited for our drugs, he would argue that molesting children was justified, as long as the child made the first move. But pot was worth it. And worth more.

Pot was the basis of many relationships. I smoked pot with Sledge every day, every two hours, for five years. We couldn't do anything without first being high. It started in the morning right after coffee. We'd jack up high as kites on caffeine just so we could surf on the head waves with hits off his bronze bat, a small pipe that could be easily concealed in a clever pot box or your front pocket. It looked a little like a miniature cigarette holder. After getting sufficiently high, we'd laugh or make mixed tapes or go shopping or try to write or get more coffee to get wired again. Sledge would get up early because he was a shame-based stoner. He didn't like what he was doing, so he had to try to deny it as much as possible. His pockets and black nylon gay man-purse were filled with stony accoutrements: mints, eye drops, gum and lip balm, an arsenal of products to cover up the tell-tale signs. I got up early, too, and we'd get together at his Castro Street apartment right away. If the phone rang, we let the voice mail get it. We'd be burnt to a crisp by 4 P.M. and need the sludgy, silty coffee from Café Flore to jolt us back into the world of the living. I hate that time of my life and I hate Sledge now so much for making all that waste seem like so much fun. I wasted so much of my life just walking around high and shopping, and if I were to do it all again, I wouldn't, and that is the truth. Yet I had so many chances to get away from pot addiction and I always went back. I couldn't help myself. I didn't have to buy the drugs anymore. Sledge had the dealer. And I didn't have to be high alone anymore. I had my drug buddy. We ruled the Castro and smoked and ate and smoked and ate and ate well into the night. I always felt fat, but now I felt fatter.

Sometimes, we did Ecstasy, which was good because it would help me lose weight, if only for a day. I think one of the reasons I was so attached to Sledge is that he always told me that I was pretty and thin. I needed that then as much as I needed being high. He was my most frustrating friend but also one of the closest and the hardest to give up—just like pot. Pot will make you go insane, eventually. It also makes you hungry. I remember countless stony feasts up at Sledge's apartment. He had this foodie boyfriend for a while who'd make us real Caesar salads, where he would actually rub the bowl with a piece of cut garlic. That was the gayest thing I have ever seen.

We would sit in the kitchen and watch him seasoning that big wooden bowl, and pass joint after joint after joint, and then pass thin slices of salami wrapped around hunks of cream cheese, which we would swallow whole between tokes. I think we were looking to bombard all the senses at the same time. First, the "Sledgehammer"—choking, nasty hits of green, sticky bud—and then trying to retrieve yourself from the Great Green Beyond with the creamy, crunchy, chewy, pungent, subtly sweet everything of food that never seemed to stop coming. Each new dish appeared with a collective groan and a sigh as if the expulsion of air would create more room in our bulging bellies crammed full with escape and bread.

After that, there would be more pot to make you forget the pain of overeating—and to make you want more, even though you are not sure if your body can take it. Then, eating again to take away the guilt of the eating in the first place. Sledge was so thin. I thought I'd be okay. I thought I could do it if he could do it. He told me I was thin. He told me it was okay. But it wasn't.

Comedy helped me pull away from this self-destruction, at least at the beginning.

It gave me something to look forward to, besides the constant state of numbness that had been my only pursuit. I couldn't be too high when I performed. I was paranoid enough onstage. Trying to do it high was impossible.

My first performance in a comedy club was with Batwing Lubricant, my high school improv group. We did a showcase night at the Other Café, the legendary comedy club in the Haight, where performers like Robin Williams, Paula Poundstone, and Bobcat Goldthwaite regularly took the stage. We killed and were invited back for another night. The comics hated us because we were so young and cocky, but that didn't take away from what was a life-changing experience for me.

I saw, in that dark and smoky club, the rest of my life. I thought if I could just be allowed to go onstage and make people laugh every night that I wouldn't care if I made money or became famous. Just the ability to do it would be payment enough. I don't know if I feel that way anymore. I have become jaded in my own way, and I love the material success that I have been so lucky to receive, but the way it all started was with my intense love of comedy and everything that went with it.

It wasn't easy in the beginning. The other comics were suspicious of newcomers, and I was scared of most of them. I would go to the Sunday Showcase at the Punchline, where the local acts ruled the stage, and I watched and learned from the masters. On a good night you could see Bobby Slayton or Will Durst, and at the Other Café, you could go watch Paula Poundstone. Rick Reynolds ruled the Improv, and in those early days, I went to shows like I should have been going to class.

Comedy was all I ever wanted. When I began, I don't think anyone believed I would go anywhere. After I dropped out of the School of the Arts in my senior year to do drugs and go to Europe, it was no surprise that I didn't end up getting into college. My parents lied and told their friends that I was living in the dorms, when in reality I was frying my brains out on LSD in Amsterdam. I came home in a black mood, drug weary and confused about what to do with my life. Comedy was the answer, and my indecision became resolve. During the day, I worked at my parents' bookstore with Dante and Forbes, and at night I would prowl the clubs, trying to get in, trying to get on. I didn't do as many drugs, because I had something outside myself to focus on. This comedy obsession pulled me out of a major depression. Going to clubs gave me something to look forward to. It showed me there was a life after school. My glory days were not over. They were just beginning.

My parents did not understand, of course. They never even came to see me perform. They finally saw my show once last year. Even then it was a struggle! In the very early days, I would urge Trace and AJ and Duncan to come to the Rose and Thistle to see me. After the shows, on the car ride home, there would be long, uncomfortable silences, followed by a "Wow, it's really brave of you to get up there and do that . . ." The experience of going to clubs and hanging around hoping to get noticed was terrifying. The first time I played the Punchline, I was worried I'd have to pay to get in. I was afraid to go into the greenroom because the other comics were in there. All these grown men seemed to be having such a good time with each other, and they had staked out that territory for themselves. They sat around in that holy room smoking, laughing, talking about how bad the crowd was, and patting each other on the back for a job well done.

I just hung around the closed door, not part of the audience, not one of the performers. No one took me under their wing, no one knew I existed. My invisibility wasn't particularly painful, because it was just like everywhere else in my life, but I was determined here to change all that. If I didn't enter the greenroom, I didn't act as if I was scared to, I just pretended to myself that I didn't want to, and that standing by the door was where it was at.

Eventually, I met other people who thought standing by the door was better, too. Before we knew it, we just fell into the greenroom when no one else was there, and suddenly that room was ours, and there were new, younger, scared people standing by the door, where we once were. I invited them in.

Stand-up comedy was so scary back then. It was okay once I actually got onstage, but the entire day before was nightmarish. I worried constantly about what I would say. I wondered what the crowd would be like or if there even would be a crowd. I was worried about the comics before me and if I could follow them. I thought about what I would say, and then got scared that I wasn't funny enough. The fear brought on a panic of whether I was kidding myself or not. I asked myself why I was doing this in the first place, putting myself through all this. What would happen if I forgot all my material? What would happen if I accidentally stole material from somebody else without even knowing it and got a reputation as a thief? What would happen if for some reason I was unable to get to the club? Would I be able to call them and tell them I wasn't coming? What if I just called and said I couldn't do it? What if I just told them that I was sick and woke up not funny and my dog ate my jokes, and what would happen what would happen what would happen. . . . It would reach a boiling point when I got to the club, then it simmered throughout the night until finally my name was called and I would walk onto the stage. I'd stand by the bar or by the stage entrance and my back would get all cold and my spine would tingle, my hands would shake and I wouldn't be able to concentrate on anything or who was performing at the moment. I just wanted to run away, and then suddenly, the emcee would say my name and I would miraculously walk out on my own two feet and get the first joke out.

Most of the time, it would go fine, and people would laugh and I'd stand a little taller and feel a little more confident. Sometimes, I wasn't very good. Time would drag and I'd leave the stage defeated, but it never felt as bad as I thought it would. Afterward, I would try to get back on stage as soon as possible, to erase what I had done, to get some kind of performance retribution.

I did comedy for many years in San Francisco, living out the rest of my teens in the clubs and one-nighters all around the Bay Area. In addition to that, I worked at FAO Schwarz, did phone sex, and worked at my parents' bookstore all at the same time to support my comedy habit. FAO Schwarz was the most corporate job I'd ever had, and every day I would dress up in a red yarn wig and bloomers and pass myself off to the bratty kids as Raggedy Ann. One kid kicked me and said emphatically, "Raggedy Ann is not Chinese!" I spent my breaks with the Toy Soldier getting high on the top floor of the parking garage across the street.

I would get off work at FAO Schwarz and rush over to the phone sex job. Usually, I didn't have time to change in between, so I would be doing phone sex still dressed as Raggedy Ann.

I got the phone sex job from a dumpy, aspiring actress named Kiley, who helped other dumpy, aspiring actresses get entry-level positions in the sex industry (no pun intended). This was in the halcyon days of phone sex recorded messages, before the advent of *Girl 6* and the Internet. We would get paid about $10 per message, and each was only about a minute long, so it was a good job. You got even more money if you were willing to write your own scripts. I felt like Anaïs Nin, writing erotica for my supper.

The downside was you had to be in the glass recording booth with the creepy technician, Maslowe, a smallish man with red curly hair all over his chest, spilling out in tufts from his open pirate shirt. He wore knee-high boots with khaki riding jodhpurs tucked into them, so he looked even shorter than he was, and somehow, I picture him carrying a machete, although I don't believe that it was ever part of his ensemble. Since he dressed so outlandishly, he never commented on my Raggedy Ann outfit. I probably looked normal to him.

In the cramped and close quarters of the sound booth, Maslowe would sit with his boots propped up on the desk, stinking of Brut. "C'mon, make it real for me. Breathe harder, get me off. Act like you like it. You can touch yourself if you want. I don't mind."

I would try to read again, now totally self-conscious, even more wooden than before. I tried to ignore what he just said, tried to act cool, like "I'm a grown-up, I don't mind being talked to like that," but I couldn't.

Sometimes, Maslowe would give me a lollipop.

"This'll make you sound wetter. More open. Suck it."

All of his notes just made me worse, less sexy, more scared. Sometimes he would get so frustrated with me that he would tear off his headphones and leave the little booth. I'd just sit there and wait for him to come back, which he always did eventually. I think he wanted me to chase after him, so I'd find him outside on the fire escape, looking off into the distance. Then, I'd wrap my arms around him, begging him to come back. He wouldn't listen, and I'd just carry his little body back to the sound booth, apologizing profusely the entire time, and then cream into the mike like Apollonia or Vanity or some other Prince protégé.

By Jove, I think she's got it!

I never did. I just sat there. He would come back, carrying a cup of coffee, and finish recording me. Despite his "artistic" ambitions, we still had a job to do. The coffee was Maslowe's way of covering up for his tantrum under the guise of thirst.

Maslowe got fired, and Kiley took over as sound technician, which made it much easier. We got a contract to do a series of messages, called *Hot Girls USA*. It was part of *Learn English!*, an educational program for the employees of a Japanese company. Japanese men could call in and get extra credit for the language course and supposedly get off at the same time. Talk about killing two birds with one stone.

Since the messages were designed to teach English, the text had to be simple and straightforward.

"*Hello. My name is Candi. I have blonde hair. I have large breasts. I enjoy sex. My favorite activity is sucking cock. This is most enjoyable. Do you enjoy sex?*" (*space for response*)

"*Good. I like to have sex every day.*"

I made a lot of money on those sessions, and Maslowe wasn't there, so I didn't have to look at his miserable Khaki wearin' ass, or be grossed out by his controlling, sexually violating direction.

Usually after I finished at the phone sex studio, I would go to my parents' bookstore and work until closing, the red circles and brown freckles fading on my tired face. Then I'd go home and change and go to a show. I was exhausted, but so excited by the comics and the great people I was meeting and the fantastic shows I was seeing, that I went to bed every night hotly anticipating what the next day would bring.

When my parents closed the bookstore in 1987, all the employees scattered to find other bookstore jobs. I was looking for something different. I saw an ad in the San Francisco *Bay Guardian* looking for a salesperson at a lesbian SM leather boutique called Stormy Leather. It intrigued me, so I applied. I walked into the little warehouse on Howard Street, in the just-becoming-fashionable South of Market district, and I almost ran smack into a beautiful, tall blonde woman. She had a crew cut and Buddy Holly glasses. She was wearing a black leather harness and jeans. Her breasts were bare under the harness and they looked as perfect as vanilla ice cream. We looked at each other and both turned bright red as she ran back into the dressing room. I felt as if I'd come home.

The retail store was attached to the workshop, which was directly behind a big, leather curtain. Stormy Leather had recently opened the retail store, to supplement its already hugely successful mail-order business. It sold leather lingerie and sex toys to the lesbian-Pat-Califia-leather-babes of San Francisco and the sexually adventurous suburban computer power couples of Silicon Valley. The warehouse smelled pleasantly of hides and rubber dildos, and I sat behind the counter and buzzed customers in.

My sidework included interesting tasks like shining the chrome cock rings until I could see my face, making sure the bamboo canes made an ominous sound as they whipped through the air, dusting latex fetish garments with baby powder, and putting fresh batteries into vibrators. I spent hours creating fabulous displays for butt plugs. I really let the Muse take over.

The clientele was very polite, and ever so happy to be spending their money on what they loved to do. SM is a wonderful hobby for many, and those that have the time and the finances to collect the pricey gear are lucky and know it.

Stormy Leather carried an impressive array of leather and fetish equipment, and I learned so much about what people can do in bed. I also got to experience some things firsthand.

I got invited to an SM play party sponsored by a club called Links, which catered to the gay-les-bi-transgender SM community. I'd been working at the store for about a year and had never played myself, outside of beating this guy with a riding crop. The experience for me wasn't exactly sexual. He got on my nerves, and then he wouldn't stop calling me! I knew there was enormous power in that kind of sexuality, and I was curious to see what people actually did after they bought all the stuff.

I went with another girl who worked at the store, Jadine, and her boyfriend Ian. It was held at a computer magnate's house in Bernal Heights, and there was a canned food drive that night, offering money off the price of admission with a donation of canned goods. We saw a mistress walk in with a slave on a leash in one hand, and a can of Dinty Moore Beef Stew in the other.

We paid our admission and walked into the party. The house was *Sunset*-magazine-style-Californian, with lots of redwood decks and Adirondack chairs. Some leather-dykes hovered around a sorry buffet of Granny Goose potato chips and onion dip, laid out on paper plates, with Cragmont soda in two-liter bottles. The smell of hot dogs filled the room, but the mysterious sausages were nowhere in sight. For some reason, the food at the sex parties is always terrible. I suppose this is to encourage the guests to eat each other, rather than the hors d'oeuvres.

Jadine and Ian went off to explore the house. I sat down in the living room and tried to look comfortable in my black vinyl catsuit. A youngish, Filipino woman knelt at my feet. She wore Dickies and a leather cap, which she gallantly pulled off her head while addressing me. She said, "My mistress has given me permission to kiss your hand. May I kiss your hand?"

"Uh. Yeah. Sure. Whatever."

I was being so uncool.

I excused myself as fast as I could and went downstairs into the dungeon. I ran down and found Jadine and Ian sitting in the corner. Lots of people were milling about, older couples in leather and latex, mean little lesbians in tight, dirty jeans, some drag queens—but nobody was really doing anything. It was just like being at a school dance where nobody wants to dance first, and everybody is acting like they are too bored or too tired, or they don't have time just yet, but maybe later.

Suddenly, a very fat woman walked out to the center of the party. About five of the mean-looking leather girls tackled her to the floor. Her massive body came crashing down, and they tore off her muumuu and began an intense rape scene, pulling her legs apart and roughly inserting a bright orange dildo that looked like a safety cone into her vagina.

Jadine and Ian ran out of the party. As they went by, I think I heard her mumble a Doppler-effected "Really exhausted, gotta go . . ." but she was moving too fast. I couldn't move. I immediately thought I should try to help this woman, and I couldn't understand why nobody was helping her. I thought I should call the police. Then, I remembered where I was.

Almost immediately, everyone around me, all the SM wallflowers, sprung into action. The ice was certainly broken! An older man in a leather codpiece came over and sat by me on the bench. "Don't you work at Stormy Leather?"

"Yes. I do. Hi. I'm Margaret."

"Yeah. Do you remember me? You sold me this jockstrap."

He casually unsnapped the front of his jockstrap to reveal his soft cock and balls, nesting in the fishnet underneath like a bunch of grapes. I tried not to jump up, thinking that the proper etiquette here would be to act calm and interested. "Oh. That's, uh, that is, just *fine*."

"I'm here with my wife. Maybe you'd like to play with us? You could whip me if you'd like."

"Uh. Thanks. But I'm watching my friend's purse. I can't right now."

In the middle of the party there was an old man, around 80 or so, in leather chaps and gray handlebar mustache like an octogenarian Village Person, strapping a young boy to a table. He was applying a sewing implement, that spiked-wheel thing that resembles a pizza cutter, directly onto the boy's massive erection. The dangerous-looking wheel left behind tiny drops of blood all along the shaft. Ow ow ow ow ow ow.

It was shocking, the rape, the blood, the violence, the SM theme music ("Whip It," "Master and Servant"), yet I didn't leave. I couldn't leave. It was so fascinating. It wasn't exactly a turn-on for me, but everybody else was having such a good time, and so involved in what they were doing, the feeling was contagious. I saw that there was so much more to sex than just doing it with the lights off and hoping that you didn't get pregnant.

A small crowd gathered around a threesome, a woman, a man, and a transvestite. The woman and the transvestite wore matching blue corsets, and the man was in a leather codpiece. The woman was suspended in a leather hammock and she was lying with her back against the man. She leaned her head back and looked deeply into his eyes while being vaginally fisted by the transvestite. The whole picture was quite romantic. There seemed to be so much affection between those three, and even though they were being watched by many, it still seemed intensely private, and completely beautiful. I must be pretty jaded, when seeing something like that makes me go "Awww ...," but it was something that made me understand that love is everywhere, and takes many unexpected forms. Any kind of love is fine, it's your hate you have to watch.

The party was well under way, and I noticed the woman who had been the victim of the rape scene at the beginning of the evening was now walking around collecting cups and paper plates. Later, she was fast asleep in a dark corner, snoring like she was sawing logs.

I ran into a drag queen acquaintance of mine named Nigel, and he strapped me to one of the crosses and put a scouring pad on my leg, but it was just funny, not sexy.

It's odd, but I always get recognized at the most inconvenient times. We went into the dungeon area, where there were people in cages, and one girl who was behind bars and tied up hopped over and said, "Hey! Aren't you Margaret Cho?" I was excited, because it was early enough in my career that being recognized still felt like an accomplishment. But at the same time, it was kind of weird considering where we were. Besides, she was hog-tied!

Suddenly it was late, and I was one of the last people to leave the party. I had had a great time and was looking forward to the next one. San Francisco is such a great place for sexual exploration. There are so many things to do, so many closets to come out of. It's not just a gay-straight-bi question. It really is multiple choice. The attitude is so playful and friendly, more like a sexy theme park than perversion.

I didn't get another opportunity to go to a sex party for many years. My career started to move and I was scared that these forays into alternative sexuality would somehow catch up with me. That was such a stupid idea, especially because I was talking about it on stage.

Much later in my career, when I was in the middle of *All-American Girl*, the tabloids went and took a picture of Stormy Leather's signage and told idiot readers that I had worked in a "steamy sex job," but they never explained what it was.

After my TV show was over, and I was spending a lot of time drinking and doing drugs and playing comedy clubs, I went to see a friend of mine perform in a production put on by the Til Eugelspiegel Society, New York's oldest SM organization. The theater wasn't opened up yet when I got there, so quite a few people were milling about in the lobby. I sat down on a hard bench, and soon an older woman dressed in a leather corset and very high heels teetered over to me and bent over. She got uncomfortably close to me, and I wanted to move, but I didn't want to be rude. Her lover, a gruff mature man wearing a menacing-looking bullwhip on his hip, snapped a wooden cane over the woman's rear, just barely missing my face.

I decided to move. Obviously they didn't care about my feelings, so why should I worry about theirs?

The theater finally opened, and we all filed in. The audience was instructed to stand in a circle and the performers walked into the center. There was a rather large assortment of characters, almost as many as were watching. There were women wearing large headdresses made of tree branches. A man and a woman, both naked, stood with their long hair woven together so they were hair Siamese twins attached at the braid. There was some chanting, and then some holding of hands and walking in a circle, and then all hell broke loose. The inner circle began to attack the outer circle. A bald man who looked just like Anthony Edwards dressed in a diaper grabbed me and demanded to see my underwear. I was so scared but didn't want to appear to be, so I remained as calm as I could, even though my period had spontaneously started and the exit sign was nowhere to be found.

I bled and bled and ran away from the *ER* diaper man. The emcee, a tall, striking-looking man in a top hat and fishnet tights, emerged from the crowd. He started to make loud demands on the inner circle. "I want a cowardly man! Bring unto me a lily-livered coward." A nerdy guy clutching a Tower Records bag was snatched up by a girl with antlers and brought to the center of the room.

"Bring me a pair of young lovers!" My two friends from the lobby were thrown into the center of the room. I bled and bled, but things started to get fun. It was kind of hilarious, all of this posturing, this pagan ritual with a bunch of art students, career nerds, and bridge-and-tunnel swingers. I pulled away slightly from the circles and leaned against the wall.

Suddenly, the emcee screamed, "Bring me a fat woman! I want a fat woman now!!!!!"

It was as if everything stopped, and the entire room turned to face me.

"Who—me? No no no no!!!"

The *ER* diaper man grabbed me and dragged me over to the emcee, who was wearing a lipstick smile from ear to ear. I was horrified, and bleeding harder than ever and yelling, "But I'm not fat! Hey!!! I am not fat!!!!!"

The emcee tossed his head back and cackled like a scary witch. "No. She's not fat. Just a little bit chubby!" With that he grabbed a handful of my stomach and shook it. I would have started crying, but the lights suddenly came up, and all the players vanished, leaving the entire audience breathless and somewhat red in the face. I shook myself off, pulled in my pretty-flat-stomach-considering even further, and tried to leave the premises as quickly as possible. I didn't care about seeing my friend. I would explain later, having more than enough of an excuse.

Right before I got out the door, the nerdy guy with the Tower Records bag caught my arm and said, "Hey, aren't you Margaret Cho?"

9

WHY YES, I AM MARGARET

"You came offstage, this was at the Punchline in San Francisco, and I said, 'Good set.' And you said 'Thanks' and then you goosed me," Paul said.

I honestly didn't remember that, but Paul insisted that it was true. He came to the Laugh Factory recently to see me. When I walked into the club, I saw his face and distantly remembered it but I couldn't place it. I couldn't imagine ever goosing anyone, but I took his word for it. At that time, I was just learning how to be an outrageous diva, so there were quite a few missteps along the way. Goosing people, pink wigs, and rhinestone bow ties all play a part in my humble beginnings. It took some time to let my own style emerge. I was brainwashed by the female comics of the '80s, and felt compelled to wear shoulder pads and to be a bawdy, wisecrackin' broad.

Paul and I were both working the road gigs all over California in the late '80s. There was a chain of restaurants called the Sweetriver Saloons that had comedy on the weekends, so every Friday, comics would drive to Eureka, Santa Rosa, Pleasanton, and Merced for the shows.

Merced was the worst. Not only was it a three-hour drive, you had to stay at the Happy Inn, which was anything but. It seemed like a lot of suicides happened there. Even so, there was no death quite as painful as the one you would die onstage that night, as the Merced intelligencia would congregate around potato skins and daiquiris and judge your comedy and your city ways.

Ed Marques and I played it once, and we laughed and kept the doors to our Unhappy rooms open because they wouldn't close all the way anyway. The road could be fun sometimes and the Sweet-rivers were good gigs because we were paid well ($50 per show), and we were given a food ticket worth $12. That could be two meals if you were savvy, and we were in those days.

I did all those one-nighters and stayed in all those crappy motels and drove a million miles and stuffed the loneliness with food and pot and dreams that maybe this would all lead to something.

I don't reminisce often about the days when I would do my best fifteen minutes for a bunch of drunks in suburbia. It felt good to do it, but it felt better to be done.

Paul reminded me that my success did not happen overnight. It took so many years of working the road, hoping for those occasional TV spots, deals that were made and that never went through and op-portunities lost and found to get to where I am today.

The night he came to see me was typical of the legendary Saturday nights on the Sunset Strip, where the "big boys" play. These prime headliner slots at the club on the weekends, when the crowd is pumped and every young comic is champing at the bit to get on, were all I ever dreamed of as I was coming up. I wanted to come to the big city and kill. I knew that it was possible, someday. Now, the day has come, and I appreciate every second of it.

I went onstage and remembered all the sorrowful nights at the Sweetriver Saloons when I couldn't buy a laugh from the stupid crowd. That night, so many years later at the Laugh Factory, I killed the audience. They were laughing so hard the room was shaking. I got so high from it—*this is my life and this is what I do best.* I came offstage thinking my best fifteen minutes got so much better after ten years.

When the crowd is with you, the jokes are fresh, your timing is just right, and the moon is in the seventh house and Jupiter aligns with Mars. You feel like you are exactly where you should be, and there is nothing better. Comedy is a rare gift from the gods, an awesome invention. It propels you right into the heart of the universe.

No wonder all the great comedians had such destructive private lives. Lenny Bruce had to shoot up, Richard Pryor had to freebase. Sam Kinison was just as abusive towards himself as he was to the crowd. After you get the audience into that kind of frenzy, and you are being worshiped like the false idol you are, how do you leave the stage and transition back into real life? How can you just come down? How can you ease back into mortality? What will you do for an encore? What is there left to do but set yourself on fire?

I went home. I left my old acquaintance Paul and thought about what a little girl I used to be onstage, and how I grew up there. I remembered how I wore long black gloves with little red bows on them. I remembered the times I tried and failed and bombed so very bad. I remembered how I tried to sleep in the barren and desolate motel rooms after. I remembered how my face would burn when I was up onstage, working hard but hardly working. I remembered what I wanted to be when I grew up, and realized I had become just that.

Most comedians say that the best thing that you can hope for as a comic is to have your own sitcom. This is the top. This means you have "made it." It is supposedly what we all aspire to. I guess this was what I wanted, too, but I never really thought about the work that it would entail. I believed being rich and famous would somehow take care of all that for me.

I thought that I would innately know what to do, and even if I didn't, I'd have many shrewd advisers. I pictured myself sitting on the set, in a crisp white shirt and a black leotard, straddling my folding chair, and barking out orders to yes-men as I dragged deeply on a Chesterfield. I'd spend my nights getting to parties late, and drag my faux fur across the floors of crowded rooms. I'd throw my head back when I laughed, have orgasms from intercourse, win Emmys and deliver acceptance speeches while prettily holding back tears. I'd receive diamond necklaces from millionaire suitors and give them to my friends, like Madonna in that video. I'd enjoy being a girl and ultimately become the beautiful swan I knew I was inside.

Not having a clear vision of what I wanted from this business, aside from these fantasies of the glamorous life ("Hills that is, swimming pools, movie stars . . ."), I just started saying I wanted what everyone else wanted. Looking back, I realize this was my biggest mistake.

We must know who we are, so we can know what we want, so we don't end up wanting the wrong thing and get it and realize we don't want it, because by then it is too late. We are powerful enough that we can manifest anything into our lives. To use this power with great care and love is the secret to living a happy life. I wish I had known this then.

I moved to Hollywood around the time when stand-up comics were being sought out for sitcoms. The successes of Seinfeld and Roseanne paved the way for many would-be stars like me. For a few years I had been working on the road and accumulating television credits here and there. My *Evening at the Improv* and MTV credentials got me a tiny bit of notice. I even got to be on *Star Search*.

It wasn't regular *Star Search*, it was *Star Search International*, this ghetto version of the show where they would put all the performers that were foreigners, or at the very least, not white. The prize money was significantly reduced, and you got to compete in only one round. The comic from India got a booking and had to be replaced by some guy from Canada, which I thought was really pushing the "foreign" angle. I was representing Korea! This was ridiculous because I was born here and I am probably more American than most people. The talent coordinator for the show knew this, and actually asked me if I could make my act more "authentic."

"Could you be more, oh I don't know, *Chinese*?"

"I'm Korean."

"Whatever."

What was I supposed to say?

"My husband is so fat, that when he sit around the *habuku*—he really sit around the *habuku*!"

They even put the Korean flag up next to my name on the bottom of the screen while I was performing. It was kind of like being in the Olympics without the medals or the endorsements. Not winning was nothing compared to the disappointment of not getting to compete on the real show.

All my comic friends got to be on "real" *Star Search*. All my comic friends seemed to be able to do whatever they wanted. Having to factor in the color of my skin whenever I tried to do anything really frustrated me. It is not that I was ashamed of my background, but that was all anybody could see at first. That was the real difference between performing stand-up in the clubs and trying to make it in L.A.

On the circuit, all the comics were judged by how funny you were. That was it. Of course, the few times I got heckled, it was race related—"Open your eyes!" and "Me so horny!" and of course the old standby, "Godzilla!," but there is nothing a good "Do I go to where you work and slap the dick out of your mouth?" can't fix. Now, in L.A., there were no clever comebacks, because there were no opportunities for them.

It wasn't always about race. Once, *The Montel Williams Show* had up-and-coming comedians on, and I was booked with lots of other comics. The makeup guy took one look at me and rolled his eyes. He hit my nose a couple of times with a sponge and told me to get out of his chair.

Then this tall, gorgeous, exotic-looking brunette who used to be a model and was now trying stand-up comedy sat in my place. He spent almost an hour and a half with her, separating her long eyelashes with a pin, delicately shading her lovely features so the camera could capture her beauty to full advantage. Then he ended up following her for the rest of the afternoon with a brush and powder, so that he could matte her down the second he saw a bead of perspiration form on her captivating visage.

This hurt me very much until that girl performed later and she was not funny at all. She was still beautiful, but she bombed so badly she became ugly by proxy. I did really well and was glad that I didn't have to wash off all that shit anyway.

That makeup artist worked on my TV show years later. I recognized him instantly and the entire time we worked together I did not look at him or even speak to him once. Everybody thought it was the typical behavior of a bitchy Hollywood star, and I just let them all think that. I did not believe I had to explain myself. As immature and bitter as that is, at least I didn't have him fired. He just served as a constant reminder to me that I wasn't pretty enough. I would do things like that to abuse myself in those days. It was my fault for not being enough, I thought, but it was his fault for being an asshole. Plus—he was straight! What the fuck is that? Never trust a straight guy who does makeup unless he does the aliens on *Star Trek*.

When I got my sitcom development deal, it was more than just money that I got from it. It gave me a sense of power and self-esteem that I desperately needed at the time. Working in Hollywood, and not being traditionally beautiful or tall or skinny or blonde or even a guy, I felt invisible a lot of the time. It was depressing to be in casting offices with the best-looking people in the world, fighting it out for a walk-on role in *The Red Shoe Diaries* (even though I did wind up getting that part). I felt sexless, useless, ugly and fat, and had no idea how I was going to get past my physical self and show the producers that I actually had a lot of talent.

Once, I went to audition for some shitty science fiction movie. I went into the office with as much confidence as I could muster. I had spent many hours in careful preparation, learning my lines, really thinking about this part. I figured since I didn't have the looks (whatever that meant), at least I could work at it and maybe that would pay off somehow.

It was one of those hot Southern California days where the smog is thick and magnifies the sun's rays. Driving across town in the miserable heat with no air conditioning in my aged Volkswagen Golf seemed to melt my confidence along with my makeup. The casting agent's office was shady and cool. There was this male model reading with me. As I read, I was consumed by the part. I was Commander Rina, and we were low on fuel and I was determined to get us off the planet before the dust storm damaged my ship. I finished and looked up at the casting agent. She sighed and looked at me with disgust.

"Don't you ever go into another audition and give a reading like that again. I suggest you go take some acting classes at once. I am only telling you this for your own good. Don't you ever ever ever. Now thank you. Please leave."

The male model just sat there and smirked at me the whole time. When I shut the door behind me, I could hear them laughing.

Actors face that kind of rejection every day. The experience was upsetting, but it did not keep me from trying. I knew there was something better out there for me, and that if I kept going that I would be rewarded for my efforts. Why was I so tough? It was because I wasn't just looking for a job, I was looking for some self-worth. I constantly looked outside myself for something that would *fix* me, and it was a desperate search.

This need to avenge myself upon all the casting directors, producers, actors, makeup artists, agents, and assholes who said I couldn't do it, who denied me my need for validation, was a big motivation. My values were all screwed up. Looking for self-esteem outside myself and thinking I could find it in Hollywood was insane, but I didn't know any better at the time. I thought if I could get the job, get noticed, maybe even become a star, then I would stop hating myself, and adore me just like the rest of the world. Self-love doesn't work like that. Life doesn't work like that.

I had thought for so long that it was somehow noble to hate myself. As if fate would take kindly to me, and say, "You adorable little scamp! Somebody will love you, because you just can't seem to!" Then, it was a matter of wanting people to love me, despite the fact that I could not love myself.

I knew this girl who seemingly hated herself, and yet she was beautiful and men fell at her feet while she did her best to seem insecure. Now, I think it was all an act. It was not possible for her to hate herself as much as she said she did and still have that kind of pulling power. She'd say, "I am so unattractive . . ." and bat her violet eyes in such a way that young men would swoop down around her to convince her otherwise.

I think that I said things like that about myself hoping for the same response. I wanted people to shake their heads sadly and think, "She has no idea how beautiful she is . . ." and sigh at the irony of life.

Unfortunately, when I said, "I am so fat" and didn't immediately get a response like "No you're not!" I felt like the other person had just agreed I was fat. Their nonparticipation in my make-believe dialogue made me resentful, without them having done anything.

It would be worse if they decided to joke along with me. I remember working on a film with an aging actress, and every time I put myself down and called myself fat, her face would fill with orgiastic delight. She was so excited to go down that path with me and criticize my body, as long as I was instigating it, of course. I guess she wanted me to see that she could be as mean to me as I was, and do it all in the name of good fun.

Ultimately, other people are amateurs compared to me in the horrible things I can say about myself. I cannot even bear to list the things that fill my mind during these episodes of self-loathing. I think we all have our own messages, the tapes that play over and over in our minds, that weaken us, that desecrate the holiness of our lives, that come disguised as a way to motivate ourselves, when really they are all about self-sabotage.

I don't want to be weary anymore. I don't want to be my own worst enemy anymore. When I tell myself I am fat, that I have to work out, I've taken from myself the energy to go out and do it. I feel hurt, bled of life force, and then I must work with that deficit. I give up before I am through because I feel defeated before I even begin.

Self-hatred doesn't accomplish anything. It destroys everything it touches, comments upon, attacks, judges. No great deity is going to come to you, in those great moments of self-loathing, and rub the dirt from your rosy hobo cheeks and say, "Chin up! It's not so bad!" I think that was what I was always hoping for, that God would try to prove me wrong; if I hurt myself enough, God would try to stop it. As ridiculous as that sounds, I find that even now after admitting it, it is very hard to let go of that notion.

But I will if you will. Let's not hate ourselves. We are all we have. We cannot change anything until we accept that. I cannot do this alone. I don't love myself enough to do it alone, but I can do it if we have a pact, if I am keeping up my end of the bargain.

I have been a longtime perpetrator of hate crimes against myself, and I am turning myself in. I have had enough.

10

ROAD

By 1992, I was living in torment in L.A., only to leave for a worse life on tour.

I was eating dinner out of vending machines, spending lost hours driving on black ice all over the Northeast, performing for college kids by day, staving off the loneliness of the long-distance traveler with Sweetheart soap and red Washington apples.

In West Virginia, there were anonymous phone calls warning me that I would be spending the night in a Ku Klux Klan stronghold. In Macon, Georgia, someone tried to break into my motel room while I was sleeping. My screams set off peals of hillbilly laughter and then sudden silence. I moved all the furniture up against the door and called the unoccupied front desk all night long.

In eastern Pennsylvania, I got wrong directions that led me six hours away from my destination, and I had to backtrack hundreds of miles in the snow and ice at breakneck speed to get to the show on time. That same winter, I spent three days in the Baltimore airport under ten feet of snow to get to an all-boys' school—a military academy in New Mexico, where cadets ran onstage and did pushups in the middle of my act. I went to hell and back in the name of comedy.

There were small signs that I was starting to go insane. I rarely changed clothes or showered, sometimes for as long as two weeks. Sleeping in what I wore all day, pulling my greasy hair up with a Goody barrette, thinking it didn't matter, nothing mattered, because nobody cared.

I slept as much as I could, because that was my only escape. I got used to waking up with a too-much-sleep headache and having no idea where I was. I did this to make up for so much lost sleep, from going back and forth between time zones and losing and gaining hours every day.

Being on a tight schedule, I was terrified of oversleeping and missing flights, so I was never able to relax. Sometimes when I was home, I would wake up in the middle of the night, convinced that I was late for a flight. I would hurriedly gather my bags, which were always packed, and get dressed in the dark, only to realize when I was almost out the door that it was my day off.

Being alone all the time began to take its toll. Once, I treated myself to a fancy dinner at a hotel restaurant. The dining room was lit with candles, and filled with couples enjoying a romantic evening. Sitting alone, waiting for my lemon sole, I got bored and took out my makeup bag and started plucking my eyebrows at the table. The waiter gave me such a look of horror as he set down my overdone fish that I immediately put away my Tweezerman in shame. It was time to go home.

This was not what I had signed up for. What use was it to follow your dreams if you only wound up miserable? I wanted to be a comedian, not a traveling salesman, but that was essentially what I had become, lunging for the last Eggo waffle at the complimentary continental breakfast at the Comfort Inn in Peoria.

I still travel extensively for my work now, and I am writing these words in a hotel room. Today, I could not face another stinky, sticky hotel "health club," climbing onto rattling, ancient machines at my own risk, so I just took a shower instead. I know I should be grateful for those nasty-ass exercise rooms.

I remember when I would stay at places that didn't even have those human-salt-covered stationary bikes. For recreation, I would walk in straight lines across dry, weedy fields. Any vacant lot was my gym in those days, and I would chap rather than sweat from the wind whipping my face.

This morning, I sat in a rented limousine, on I-95, with interior colored lights changing every five seconds for my pleasure, lest I get bored on my way to the airport. It is a far cry from the rented Sunbird I used to drive on this highway, looking for exits that did not exist. Back then I prayed that I might die before the next gig, that God would just take me, because I was so tired and I just couldn't do it anymore.

I kept going. And slowly I became glad to have lived so that I could tell the tale.

I remember driving and driving to Fordham University, a school supposedly not far from where I had begun my trip in New York City. Getting to the Bronx seemed easy enough.

Fordham wasn't hard to find, since the outside of the campus was covered in barbed wire. I looked around the school for the hotel where I was supposed to be staying. There didn't seem to be one around, so I kept driving.

The streets looked dangerous, but I kept telling myself it was the middle of the day, it would certainly be all right, I was in a car after all, and I could find everything on my own. Finally, after much searching, I pulled into a motel on a side street. The place looked okay from the outside, so I parked and handed the manager seventy dollars, a fortune back then, and got the key. I walked up the rickety stairs and into my room. The door opened much too easily for my comfort, the lock nearly falling out of the rotting wood. My heart sank as I viewed the graffiti spray-painted all over the room.

I tried to reason with myself, live with it for just a second. Then, I fast-forwarded in my head to scenes of the rest of the night, like a hideous coming attraction. I saw myself going to bed, listening to gunshots and praying that I would not get shot during the night, watching the sun come up through that broken window if I was allowed to live, of course. Then, suddenly thinking, "Hey, I am getting what I asked for. I am supposed to die *this* way!"

I lugged my bags back down to the office and the manager handed me my money back right away. He hadn't even put it in the register. He knew I'd be coming back. I drove on and on, not seeing anything on the sides of the road. I had to go to the bathroom, I had to rest for just a minute, I needed a place to stop, collect my thoughts, hopefully before the show.

There had been a vague mention by the booking agent that I would be staying at a Holiday Inn, just off the highway. I searched and searched, up and down for hours, and the friendly green sign never appeared. Finally, I spotted a motel that looked fairly decent and clean on the side of the road. Thanking my lucky stars, I pulled off the freeway and into the parking lot.

The office was behind bulletproof glass once again, yet I still tried to hang onto my hopes. Most of all, I was starving, and I wanted a clean bed and room service before having to perform for the kids at the college. It seemed I had found it at last.

The man in the office was enormous and his rolls of fat pressed up against the glass. His flesh so resembled an octopus' in an aquarium, that only out of desire for a decent room could I resist the overwhelming urge to tap on the glass.

The octopus demanded payment in cash, the standard seventy dollars, before he would even look at me. He handed over the key and

I walked up the stairs, hopeful and happy, not thinking that I could have possibly made a second mistake. Why did I think I couldn't fail to find shelter twice? Why was I so confident when I opened that door?

The room was dark, as only one light was working. It stank of that weird ammonia they use to clean porno booths and strip clubs. The cherry ammonia scent is so powerful, it flavors all the drinks from the bar. I wonder if for some people it is an aphrodisiac. For me, it brought on another brief vision of being haunted by the ghosts of dead hookers and murderous johns, that porn smell permeating my luggage and my clothes for the rest of the trip, for the rest of my life.

Brave from the last motel experience, I stomped back down to the office, demanding my money back. The octopus screamed that I couldn't have a refund, then finally lifted one of his eight arms and threw thirty-five dollars back in my face.

I got back in the rental car and cried for a moment. I felt hopeless. I had to get back to the school soon. The show was about to begin. I had lost half my money for the night. I was homeless, tired, hungry. There was nothing left to do but go to the show and throw myself at the mercy of the students. At the campus, I explained my situation to the kids. They apologized profusely, although I think there was no true way for me to convey my anguish. "Sorry" was not enough for me. I wanted some kind of hotel/motel revenge. I wanted them to make it up to me and bring me to a five-star hotel, with butlers holding forth great silver platters full of Turkish Delight, after which I could fall asleep on a stack of mattresses concealing a single pea. All they did was offer correct directions back to the Holiday Inn and a caravan to ensure I arrived safe and sound.

Performing in the cafeteria to a handful of bored students trying to eat their fruit cocktail in peace was not a delightful experience either, but I was comforted that at least it was a hell with which I was already quite familiar. After the show, proper directions to the Holiday Inn in hand, I left the university. No caravan materialized, but I felt confident about finding it, since I had been going up and down that freeway all day. In my excitement, the heady, sweet thought that my search for a home might be over, I got lost trying to find the freeway entrance.

Turning down dead-end streets, driving by trash cans set ablaze and gangs of roving homeless people, I knew I was one of them. I would stop the car at an intersection and they would circle around me, shuffling their Hefty-bag tunics, trying to claim me as their own. I grew dismally aware that this might indeed be my last night on earth.

Fortunately, having had a short reprieve with the awful show, and dying another way entirely, I was determined to live. I would live to see the friendly green sign off the road. I would live to see the clean sheets of the graffiti-and-porn-smell-free room that was my birthright.

The strength of my hope got me to the freeway safely. I found the Holiday Inn just beyond the exit where earlier I had given up and turned around. I had been so close and yet so far. I almost kissed the concierge and ordered a fatted calf from room service just ten minutes before closing.

Slipping between those sheets that night, I felt a deep happiness I think I have never known before or since. Maybe that is why I have not given up traveling, even though things like this are bound to happen at every turn. The rewards are worth it. But back then, all I wanted was a way out.

I hit another low point sitting in a combination gas station/restaurant in the middle of Indiana. I hadn't talked to anyone for days except for doing the shows. It was six below zero and I'd just gotten kicked out of my motel for asking for another blanket because it was freezing.

The crazy manager of the motel was convinced that I was harboring criminals. It was my twenty-third birthday, and I was determined to celebrate it at the gas station/restaurant. All the farmers stared at me as I sat at the counter in a huge leopard-skin coat and Jackie O sunglasses eating watery chili. Clumsily, I tried to hide my self-consciousness by casually perusing a *W* magazine, but the huge pages only drew more attention to themselves. It was also depressing reading the society section, thinking about all the people in the world who were having a good time, times I could never have out here in the Midwaste.

I couldn't hold out for much longer. This was not what I had wanted for myself. I was lonely, tired and disillusioned with my career. I couldn't get any joy out of being on the road, and when I came home to auditions and casting directors, it just felt worse. Life is so terrible when you think there is nothing to look forward to. I thought that misery was my only option.

Then, something miraculous happened.

I was lucky enough to have a great agent, who not only booked me in all of the colleges I was doing, but who guided me into the world of network development.

Nothing came easy. Trying to get an agent had been a nightmare. I met with one guy who told me that he couldn't represent me because Asian people couldn't make it in this business. He assured me he had tried, he had a Chinese client once, and the failure was so painful he vowed never to make that mistake again.

Later, he represented one of the actresses on my TV show and he would come onto the set on tape days and I would be standing right next to him and he couldn't even look at me. I, of course, stared at him so much I am surprised he didn't burst into flames.

After all the hideous rejection, meeting Karen was like a dream come true. An agent gets you the jobs, and a manager guides your career. I had a manager already, making decisions with me between gigs that paid very little money. Karen, acting as agent, now brought me bigger and better jobs on the road. She also began working more in a managerial role, to the chagrin of my existing manager, Annie.

Karen told me that I had enormous talent and a very promising future. She understood the business, and her savvy got people talking about me and wanting to meet with me. We had showcases in L.A., where I performed for different network executives. Karen said that my road work was making me a great comic and that I was a sure thing.

I was suspicious of her. I could not believe that anyone would be so interested in me just for my talent. I thought she was lying when she told me I was funny and smart and that I was going to be a big star. It embarrassed me to hear her talk about me to others in such glowing terms. The audiences on the road hated me and the casting people in town hated me and most of all, I hated me. Why was she so different?

She was right, and the showcases we did started a bidding war between all the major studios. I got a deal—a great one. I am sure I would still be trying to audition for things or suffering out there on the road if it weren't for her.

Right before we did the final contracts for the deal, Annie revealed she had other plans. Annie was worried that since Karen and I were doing so much that Karen would force me to leave her behind. Annie had a tendency to be paranoid because she smoked so much pot. Since I smoked as much pot then, too, I got sucked into the drama.

Annie convinced me to take a meeting with a big agency behind Karen's back. It was doubly treacherous because Annie was staying at one of Karen's employee's apartments, blowing pot smoke out of the sliding glass doors.

I loved Karen, and I felt bad betraying her like this, but I didn't know who to trust anymore. Getting a good deal was so important. Besides, Karen's confidence in me was almost a liability because I had none in myself, and the more she praised me, the more I felt like a fraud.

The meeting with the big agency was unremarkable. They were interested, but they weren't jumping through hoops the way people did when Karen and I were in a conference room together.

Somehow, Annie let it slip about the meeting, and we were caught, agent-handed. But Karen had a plan of her own. I was in New York at the time doing a show for Comedy Central. Karen sent in Greer, a new manager from a hot firm that she knew would impress me.

Greer convinced me to leave Annie and sign with him. Karen would still be my agent, and together, he promised, we three would have the world. He took me to a swank restaurant in the Village, a place where Madonna had been recently spotted. We talked late into the night about where I would go and what I would do, now that we were together. He seduced me, not sexually, but in an emotionally intimate way. He was going to be my manager in shining armor, and I felt rescued in every sense of the word.

This was a brilliant move on Karen's part. She must have known that her words would make a deeper impression on me when spoken by a man. It is horrifying to acknowledge the sexism within yourself, because then you see the enemy is not in front of you, but behind your own eyes. The reason I didn't feel worthy of the love and support Karen gave was because she was a woman, and I couldn't trust her. I had grown up with the idea that while women may make strides without men, they could only do the real work *with* them. Even though Karen really did everything, she had to make me think it was Greer's work that was making such an impact.

I fired Annie on the telephone while she was at a New Age retreat. She started crying but was grateful for my timing because it would give her the opportunity to "share it with the group."

Greer brought me back to L.A. He seemed to work wonders on my behalf, but actually it was Karen who was making all the important decisions.

My big network deal was closing, and it seemed like things were finally starting to look up.

11

MIRACLE?

The television deal pushed me ahead of the pack. It was like I didn't have to compete anymore in a situation where I felt I was out of my league.

Even though I had no real ideas for a TV show, I thought I could be a development person of leisure, jumping from network to network, accumulating contracts and six-figure salaries, the perpetual next best thing. Greer convinced me that if it didn't work this time, we could try again and again, that there was no such thing as failure and there was no reason to be afraid of anything. He was so wrong. He just wanted the money from his big commissions. My career didn't matter to him at all, he hadn't been working on it from the beginning like Karen. He would tell me anything just to keep me happy, knowing that he could drop me if the show didn't make it, knowing that he could completely cash in on it if it did.

I called him "Dad" when we talked on the phone. I was using him, too.

I chose ABC for their historic programming—*Battle of the Network Stars, Charlie's Angels, The Love Boat, Fantasy Island*—the channel that ruled the nights of my childhood. TV was so important to me growing up. One of my earliest memories is the day I realized I was not white, and therefore not like the people I saw on TV. I was looking in the mirror and saw for the first time that the reflection was *me*. Who was this odd-looking creature with the black hair and small, black eyes? Why wasn't I like Cindy Brady? I felt like her much of the time. Why didn't my hair split neatly into blonde braids? Why were all the people on TV who looked like me foreign or ancient or fortune-tellers or servants or soldiers? Was that what people like me were supposed to grow up to be? What was the ancient Chinese secret?

It was the most alarming thing. I was really shocked that I did not look the same as my friends on the screen. I think maybe I never quite got over it—not only that I wanted to be white, but feeling that I had to correct the situation somehow.

I had a big meeting with the television executives at ABC in Century City. From the conference room windows, I looked out at the L.A. dusk. The pink clouds were dusted with orange light in the smoggy brilliance of 6 P.M., Pacific Standard Time.

Many people in the meeting hugged me and kissed my cheek warmly. I had no idea who they were. It made me tired to be the center of so much attention. I sat there while the executives droned on and on about how we were going to create this amazing hit TV show by finding the right writers and the right actors, etc., etc., etc. All I could think about was the traffic I would have to face going home. My feeling was "Why do we have to talk about it? What is there to say? Why can't we just do it?" This sitting around and theorizing about comedy doesn't make it funny; you need to be down there, in the trenches, working it out.

Plus, the executives were the most humorless, dry, intimidating people I had ever met. They were the kind of people in an audience who wince instead of laugh. We were trying to talk about comedy, but nobody laughed once in the meeting. I had bad feelings about them all; they didn't seem very nice.

But they wanted to do this show, this Asian-American family sit-com, and they wanted me to star in it. They said they loved me, that this was going to be a great show. I have to admit, I kind of felt like a child prodigy, like the Dalai Lama in a way. It was the miracle I had been waiting all my life for. I hated myself, but I thought that this show would somehow rectify that. If I got love from millions of people, then how could I still hate myself? Maybe I could be happy. Maybe this would do it for me. Maybe it was okay that I wasn't white, tall, thin, blonde, gorgeous, or a guy. Maybe my ship was coming in. Maybe I would make it okay for Asians to be on TV. Maybe I'd really be the first to do it.

I stopped being tired of the attention and brightened up. The traf-fic would be hell going home, but who cared? I was going to be a fucking superstar.

The network deal made me think my life had been saved. I had paid my dues—and then some. The endless road gigs that exhausted and depressed me, the lackluster homecomings, the rejection at audi-tions, these were now all behind me. I looked at a future so bright I had to wear shades.

With the deal finally in place, things started to heat up fast. I got a publicist who escorted me to countless photo shoots and interviews. I took meetings with writers, all guys from the Valley wearing puffy new Reeboks and baseball jackets from other TV shows they'd worked on. The *Life Goes On* guy blended into the *Wings* guy. I couldn't tell one from another.

We'd meet at Maple Drive or some other expensive lunch place, and they'd tell me they loved my tape, they wanted to do a great show, they had a girlfriend/friend/niece/manicurist/fuck who was Korean. They knew what it was all about. They would call my man-agement. They went to school/played racquetball/Vegas/shared hook-ers with Greer. They wanted to get in bed with me and the network and the studio so we could have a three-way all the way to the bank.

Greer, who greeted me every day with smiles and long hugs and baskets of muffins from Fancifull, set me up with Gary.

"He's just come off *Empty Nest* and he's hot!" Greer said. As far as I was concerned, anybody would have been fine. I just did not want to return to my old life.

Gary was really nice, a man with innocent charm. He was different from the other writers because he wasn't a sleazy, cigar-smoking story editor from the Valley. Gary was asthmatic, older, and lived in Beverly Hills. He said, "I get up at four every morning and write until ten." He spoke with such gaunt solemnity, I believed him. His jeans looked like a size twenty-four.

He took me to a cheap diner, not a trendy Beverly Hills bistro. He ordered a house salad with the dressing on the side and got to work. He tried so hard.

The waitress came by and before refilling his coffee cup asked him, "More hot?" He started giggling like a maniac, then that giggle turned into a cough, then came the grand finale of a huge throat-clearing with a nose-blow encore.

It's not his fault that he wasn't funny. As he pumped me for information about myself, I wasn't sure what to tell him. I really had no idea who I was. I just said whatever came to mind, made stuff up, none of which he used anyway.

He cranked out a pilot from five minutes of my standup, a sunny expose on what it was like to grow up a rebellious daughter in a conservative Korean household. I spared him the real story. The truth was that I lived in my parents' basement when I was twenty because my father couldn't stand the sight of me, and therefore banned me from the rest of the house, so that I peeped at the family through the cracks in the door under the stairs like *Bad Ronald*. I was unemployed and trying to kick a sick crystal meth habit by smoking huge bags of paraquat-laced marijuana and watching Nick at Night for six hours at a time. Now that's a sitcom.

We were going for prime time—a family show in the 8 o'clock time slot. We would be the first Asian-American family on television, which gave us a lot to consider. How were we going to portray ourselves? It had to be wholesome, even though I had no idea what that meant. The closest I ever got to that was being a *hole* to *some*. I've never been wholesome in my life.

I just went along with it. I thought they all knew what they were doing.

I THOUGHT THEY ALL KNEW WHAT THEY WERE DOING!!!!!!!!

There was a screen test for me set up at the studio. It was on the *Home Improvement* stage. I dressed up that day in a miniskirt and a midriff sweater with a long vest. I looked great. Success suits me, I thought.

The stage manager and the cameramen were so nice to me. I stood on the set and walked back and forth as the cameras rolled. I arrived home feeling like a tired hardworking actor, after a long day of shooting.

Then I got a panicked phone call from the producer of the show, a woman named Gail, whom I had really grown to love and trust. Gail liked to smoke cigarettes with me in secret. If Greer was my dad, Gail was my mom. She was the head of the production company slated to do the show and very powerful in a world of men. This impressed me to no end. After meetings, she would hug me hard with her solid arms, and my fears about everything, my insecurity about myself, even my self-hatred, would melt away.

When Gail called, her voice had neither the friendliness or the warmth I had come to associate with her. She was all business.

"We need to do something. . . . I have to tell you. . . . The network has a problem with you. They are concerned about the fullness of your face. You need to lose weight. I don't care what you have to do. We have two weeks before we shoot the pilot. I am so sorry but there isn't any way to make this nice. And far be it for me to say anything. . . . But this is for you, for your future. If you want your own show, if you want to be a star, you'll do it. We will do whatever we can. There is another test set up for you in a week. We told them you would lose some weight by then. And please, please, please do not wear anything that bares your midriff."

One "please" would have sufficed.

How do you keep going when someone tells you there is something wrong with your face?

"The network has a problem with you. They are concerned about the fullness of your face."

I will never forget it, as long as I live. I don't think Gail wanted to tell me. I knew the network executives were making her, because she was closest to me at the time, because she was a woman.

She was just trying to do her job, and I do not hold anything against her for that. Still, the "fullness of your face" was not even a kind euphemism. It was in no way subtle or tactful. What hurt most was that it was not a body part I could hide. There was no girdle or minimizer for your face. It is the part of you that cannot be changed or denied or altered. It is the very essence of you. How did I not want to hide my face forever?

I tried to lessen the shock of it, what it did to me. I tried to rationalize, like—"This is the big time, we are all gentlemen here, I can take it." I obviously couldn't.

My face. My face. We always hear, "Your face is your fortune," "The face that launched a thousand ships," "That face, that face, that beautiful face." Even when I would get heavier, people would at least say, "You've got such a pretty face." But not now. How did I not run and scream when the cameras were on me, to spare the world a glimpse at this huge face that could barely fit on the screen? I felt like the Elephant Man—my head, a gigantic monstrosity that I presented to the world, unavoidable because it was the very me of me.

The pain went deep. I wanted to kill my face from the inside out. At least a skull is small. A skeleton has a tiny face. I couldn't look in a mirror without feeling rage at myself—why does my face have to take up so much space? How I tried to kill that reflection! Working out to exhaustion, feeling the sweat pour out of my face, touching my cheeks and chin to feel if they had gotten smaller, hungry and weak, trying so hard to please this network that had done nothing but make me want to kill myself. Kill my face. But it isn't their fault, I told myself then. It is mine. I let myself react that way. I know there isn't anything I could have done about how I felt, and I cannot apologize for how I hurt myself. Who is there to say sorry to, except my face?

I want to say sorry now. To my face. My poor face that endured so much and only wanted to be pretty and liked and maybe loved sometimes and certainly didn't do any harm and could make people smile a lot of the time.

My poor face that would flush bright red from all the vodka and pills I downed so that I could pass out and not look at it anymore. My poor face that I could barely lift to have people see because I thought it was so *full*, so ugly, so wrong, so huge, so awful, so trying to be something it was not.

I kept having those feelings until they were just normal. They barely hurt, I was so used to them.

Years later, someone took a picture of me and I looked at it. Really looked at it. It occurred to me that yes, my face was full, but it was lovely. My eyebrows curved up inquisitively, sexy, like a '30s screen goddess. I had alabaster skin that glowed and Cupid's bow lips that shyly smiled.

My face was shaped like a heart, because through all of the injustices it endured, it still shined with love. Now I have finally learned how to love it back. The battle for self-esteem is a hard-won victory, because as human beings we tend to err on the side of self-loathing, but winning this war is the only way we can survive.

My agent, Karen, called almost immediately after I hung up with Gail. She was outraged and was urging me to pull out of the show. "Don't you see? They don't get you. You are making a big mistake. They can't ask you to lose weight. They can't do that! Don't let them do that! It isn't right. And if that is who they think you are, this show isn't going to work!"

I did the only thing I knew to do: I fired her. I didn't want to go back to auditions. I didn't want to go back out on the road. She didn't understand. Nobody did. If I could just lose some weight, then everything would be fine. I thought Karen was in my way, but that wasn't true. I was.

I got some new, "high powered" agents from William Morris. They all hugged me for too long and sat me down in conference rooms to talk about my possible future in CD-ROMs. They sent me lists of directors and got me auditions for "girlfriend" parts. I didn't book anything, but they said, "If it takes ten years, we'll do it." The expensive lunches and high-quality fag assistants bought my confidence.

The network mobilized the troops and launched a full-scale war against my body. A trainer named Vine came to my house six days a week at 7 A.M. and worked me out for four hours. It wouldn't have been so bad if he hadn't gone on and on about his show-business development ideas. He was the ultimate pain in my ass. A trainer/pitcher. I just hated him so much. Seeing him every day, having to make ridiculous small talk and act friendly while he was making me do sit-up after sit-up and trying to get his perfect pitch down to twenty-five words or less was nothing short of torture.

Now when I walk my dog in the hills by my house, I see trainers just like Vine walking with their clients and it seems unholy to me. I can always spot them because one person is heavier and the other person is stupider.

In addition to the trainer, I had this diet company deliver food to my house in creepy white bags because I obviously couldn't be trusted to make my own fatty choices. The portions were so small, it was hard to believe that people could survive on them. It also astounded me that I had been eating comparatively so much before. It was like I had been a gorilla, consuming my weight in bananas every day.

Now, everything that went into my mouth was carefully measured and monitored. When I finished my last meal of the day, I wanted to cry because I was still hungry. I drank so much water that my insides hurt and I stopped thinking about anything but food. I dreamt about eating spaghetti with ricotta cheese swirled into it and would wake up in a cold sweat, afraid I had actually eaten it.

I had a brand new body in days—but it didn't look any different to me. I couldn't see it, but everyone else could. "I hear Margaret Cho's got a hot body now." *Now?* What do you mean *now?*

I went to the Lava Lounge and a whole new school of guys was checking me out, which was totally terrifying. I don't know if they thought I was cute or that I was skinny enough now to "make the grade." Either way, it was scary and then it pissed me off, so it was unpleasant no matter how you looked at it or how it looked at you.

We started rehearsals for the pilot. I guess the network thought that my face could now fit on the screen and they wouldn't have to letterbox it.

The cast of the show was not only my fictional family, they immediately felt like my real family, too. B. D. Wong, Amy Hill, Clyde Kusatsu, Jodi Long, Judy Gold, Maddie Corman, the guest stars for the pilot—my old friends Kennedy Kabasares and Garret Wang—and I are bonded together because we made history. Garret and I are probably especially close because he endured some of my medical drama as well.

Through diet and exercise and sheer terror, I lost thirty pounds in two weeks. I got sick, big sick. My kidneys collapsed.

I was in my trailer with Garret. He played the first in my long string of on-screen romances. I had a crush on him, so kissing him on camera was especially pleasant.

I went into the little plastic bathroom and started urinating blood. I was screaming: "I am peeing blood! I am peeing blood!" and I sent Garret out to get someone. Then I got embarrassed, so I called him back in and said, "Forget it. I'll be okay."

Lost and confused and in pain, I called up Greer. I told his assistant Nancy, who pulled some strings and got me to the hospital without anyone knowing.

At the hospital, an old woman in a pink smock came in and introduced herself. "Hi. My name is Gwen. I am here to wash your vagina."

This later became one of my most popular routines, and it was all true. This woman's job struck me as so odd, and not only was she damn good at it—not like I know, really, I don't have anything to compare it to—but she wanted to personalize it by introducing herself, putting a name to the hose. Like she had read the "Techniques of Highly Effective People" and was applying them to me.

She cleaned me out and the doctor catheterized me. He then filled my bladder with water and inserted a tiny camera. We watched the *Fantastic Voyage* on the video monitor up in the corner of the room and I wondered if I could get a copy of the tape. Talk about an *Entertainment Tonight* exclusive.

Blood started to fill the screen and it was a surreal—and *painful*—moment, as I saw myself bleed internally on TV.

I didn't tell anybody about being hospitalized except for the people who were directly involved: Greer, Vine, and Nancy. I was ashamed and also afraid that they would somehow make me stop dieting. I didn't want to put that weight on again. I was terrified of losing the show and everything I had worked for. I didn't want to go back out on auditions and I really didn't want to go back out on the road. There was no other way.

I thought my life depended on my willingness to lose weight. Too many people were focusing on the size of my body for me to be able to feel comfortable *eating*. I now see how sick that was, but it seemed strangely normal then.

Deep inside, I knew that the show wasn't good, that I had gotten myself into a big mess. The jokes weren't so much stereotypical as stale. It had all turned out like *Saved By the Gong*. It was immature and unfunny, and playing an overgrown, oversize teenager was not my forte. I looked stupid, and even worse, I *knew* I looked stupid. Instead of focusing on that pain, I fell back on the old familiar pain of being unhappy with my weight. It is a pain I have had all my life and I know all the words to it. Ever since my first and last ballet recital when I was eight years old, when my father told me that I was the fattest ballerina, I have hated my body, and I have had to completely change my way of thinking to stop feeling it.

My kidneys bother me to this day, and I am sure the drinking and the drug abuse that came later didn't help. It was all because I did not take the warning signals my body was giving off then, because I wanted to be thin like the other Hollywood actresses, because the *Friends* were hot, because skeletal was in. Because I grew up never seeing Asian faces on TV, so inside I viewed myself as the recipient of some kind of special Hollywood gift that I needed to somehow repay with starvation. Because my mother went on crash diets. Because Gail had told me the network had a problem with my face. Because I got a letter from some prisoner who said he loved women with fat arms and that I had the fattest arms he had ever seen. Because, because, because . . .

It's funny, but the feeling I remember most about having to be hospitalized was relief that I wouldn't have to work out—at least on that day. Nancy called Vine and told him what happened. His reaction: "My God, I've killed her."

He knew how hard he was working me. He might have even known that it was unsafe, because I had been eating so little and was under so much pressure from the press and our shooting schedule.

Those weeks of working out and dieting and finally of illness made me weak and lifeless. I remember going to one Oscar party and all the queens were making fun of the gowns and the winner's hair ("Oooohh, that's right honey! Accessorize that nose with a part!") and I couldn't even laugh because I was so hungry and tired and staring at the taquitos the entire time.

Because of the bleeding and the catheter, it hurt like hell to pee. Every time I went to the bathroom, I was painfully reminded that I was fat, I was meant to be fat, would always be fat, and when I tried to starve myself thin, my body would rebel, fighting for its right to be fat.

I couldn't let up on myself. I thought beating myself up would burn more calories, so I did it until I reached my target heart rate.

The costume designer saw how hard this was for me and watched my changing sizes with sympathy. She said that she had a doctor who prescribed diet pills that worked like magic. His office was conveniently located just blocks from the studio.

After my initial visit, which included a blood test and a brief visit with the doctor, I never had to come in again, sending PAs from the show to pick up my meds. The pills were nasty smelling and I took them mostly on an empty stomach, feeling them grind against each other in the most horrifying way.

They gave me migraines and panic attacks. After the pilot was picked up, we would do network run-throughs, where all the executives would come down to the studio and watch us rehearse our unfunny show, and I would sweat so much I am sure they must have thought I was on drugs.

In a sense, I was living out a kind of *Valley of the Dolls* fantasy, taking uppers in the day to control my weight and make early call times, and getting stoned at night to come down from the amphetamines. The show was on the air, and I was flying alongside it. The pills were as addictive as the fame.

I worked out on the speedy high they gave me, in order to run faster, sweat more, die quicker. It is a miracle that I didn't give myself a heart attack. I stayed on the pills for years afterward, even after the FDA had them recalled, saying that people were experiencing lung and heart failure due to excessive use. I rationalized that my use was not excessive, that I could do it, that it was worth the risk, that being a few pounds lighter was worth *anything*. I wanted to be thin more than I wanted to be alive.

My appetite scared me so much that I spent years never even feeling it. I was so afraid that my own hunger was so great that I would consume everything in my path, and that if I let myself feel it, I would eat away my career, my livelihood, my attractiveness, everything I thought was important. I thought that if I could be thin, then I could be happy, but it wasn't true. I was thinner than I had ever been and totally miserable.

I smoked pot at night to calm my screaming head, but I did it as close to bedtime as possible so that I wouldn't eat when I got the munchies. I would fall into bed high and hungry, my head spinning with relief that I had not gone off my diet for one more day. When the place where I was going stopped supplying the pills, I changed doctors. I found a sleazier operation that dispensed outlawed prescriptions to the truly desperate. When you called them, the outgoing message was "If you are experiencing difficulty with the medication, hang up the phone and dial 911." For real, that was the outgoing message!

To make the contraband scripts last longer, I would ration them and take some mid-afternoon, then jog around Lake Hollywood in the hot sun, sometimes with a weird blue Jack La Lanne–style rubber belt on to encourage weight loss around the abdomen.

I took laxatives every day, experimenting with many kinds: drinks, powders, tablets, herbal remedies, good old chocolate squares of Ex-Lax. There are so many different ways to make yourself shit. Almost as many as there are ways to say "I love you."

My roommate at the time was bulimic, so our garbage can was always filled with chewed-but-not-swallowed peanut butter cookies.

One very famous actress, a yo-yo dieter from the old school, told me that she had maintained a thirty-pound weight loss by not eating after 5 P.M. and downing two shots of expensive tequila when she got hungry at night. She reported that it killed her hunger, and she had the tiny ass to prove it. She gave me a pair of her old shorts that no longer fit her; they were so small I couldn't get them past my ankles. Surely this was the answer.

Unfortunately for me, those two shots turned into an entire bottle of Patrón and then some. Soon, all my calories were going toward my alcohol consumption. Drinking killed my hunger as well as my already dwindling lust for life. On top of everything else, I smoked more than a pack of Marlboro Lights a day.

After the show had ended, and I was in the depths of my drinking and depression, I got a little walk-on part in a film. On the set, the makeup artist ran a brush through my hair and it all fell out. She trapped me in the chair and questioned me harshly about my diet. I told her about the pills, not wanting to but not sure I had a choice in the matter. She pleaded with me to stop taking them. She said she had done the same thing, and all her hair had fallen out and her tongue had turned black.

Seeing that I was unfazed, she kept dragging the brush over my scalp. My hair fell out in clumps, hitting the floor—*Plink! Plink!* She called over all the other actresses and makeup and hair people to watch my hair fall to the floor like rain. They all started up about the dangers of dieting and the pills, jumping around in the puddles of my hair, and yet it didn't stop me—even when I went home with a bald spot, a graying tongue, and a massive headache.

I just took more vitamins. I massaged my scalp once a day. *I kept taking the pills!* Why was being thin so important to me? Perhaps it had something to do with my upbringing. Koreans have weight issues.

My uncle lives in Tennessee, which is a problem in itself. Why a Korean immigrant would choose to live there is beyond me. He saw me on TV once and panicked. He called my mom with a new diet he had been on that really worked. She called me and I told her never to mention it again. She kept on, of course, and explained it to me again, as if my angry reaction was merely my way of saying: "Tell me one more time."

The diet consisted of consuming only one small bag of rice a week and chewing every bite fifty times. He also sent it to me in a letter that I received by registered mail and *had to sign for* when it was delivered. Not believing that was enough, he copied the letter and faxed it to me. I did not respond, and a couple of weeks later he called me and left it on my machine.

"You eat one bag, did you get my fax? You chew it fifty—because I send you a letter. . . . I think you need to lose some weight—didn't your mom tell you?!"

Then, when he was visiting out West with his family, he made a special trip to Los Angeles so he could come to my house and discuss the diet with me in person. I got him to leave by showing him pictures of myself at the Amsterdam Sex Museum riding a collection of penis sculptures much taller than myself. He departed, but not before grabbing my hand and begging me one last time to go on the bag-of-rice diet.

I have never been a heavy person, but for some reason, my physique drives some Korean people insane. They feel that I am too large for them to be comfortable, too large to be one of them, so they go out of their way to tell me what to do about it. It is either personal weight-loss secrets or cautionary tales about people who refused to lose weight ("And she never got married . . ." followed by a shudder). If it isn't that, it is because I have lost weight and they must comment on how much better I look. Most commonly, it is to inform me that on television I look grossly overweight, but in person, I look great.

My relatives were probably the worst to me about my weight, since they had my entire life to pester me about it. My mother and father, when they'd call me on the phone, would say, "How is your weight?" instead of "Hello." It got to be so unbearable that whenever they said it, I would immediately hang up on them and not let them speak to me unless they stopped saying it. How joyous being an adult and having no repercussions for hanging up on your parents! If you haven't done this, you haven't truly lived. Doing that was so instantly gratifying and wonderful, especially when they would call back and I would let the machine answer it and they would beg and plead to know how much I was tipping the scales at.

I have stopped attending family functions because my weight is commented on before, during, and after all events. My aunt's house is akin to a truck stop weigh station, and my sanity has required me to stop going there and break away from their judgment.

Anytime I meet a Korean person, it is most likely that we will make one of the comments I have outlined here. It is not a joke. It is not a sweeping generalization. I am finally breaking away from the rage that I feel about it, and connecting all of the experience for an objective examination. Why is this a collective obsession for so many Korean people? What do we feel about ourselves from the media, and about our image in the world? What do we believe is accomplished by regulating our young women this way? Is it out of care, true concern for the body and well-being of the soul? Is it strictly out of a sort of national pride and love for ourselves as a people that we feel the need to control exactly how we are perceived?

There is a passion that I love about Koreans, an internal heat that makes us drive ourselves harder, work long hours, sing loudly in the church choir, hold our families together as tightly here as we do in our homeland. Where does this passion turn inward, to cannibalize our own as "different," "imperfect," "fat"? Perhaps it's not particular to Koreans. Is there an element of this in all ethnic groups? Is there always an effort to keep us from expressing the diversity that is true to who we are as human beings, something that manifests itself in variations as numerous as the ones they are trying to conceal? Perhaps every culture on earth has its own method of doing this. It's not just Koreans, it's everyone. It's the world. It's just that the way it happens in my world hurts me so much.

I used to think it was just me, but I know that is not true. My mother has had a terrific eating disorder all my life, one that swings her weight up and down every year. I have so many cousins and other distantly and not so distantly related women who were and still are anorexic. I also received a letter from a young Korean girl whose carefully articulated experience was nearly a direct transcript of mine. I know that I am not alone.

During *All-American Girl*, I was exposed to the ugliness of the media, and since I sought definition and meaning from that world, I supposed I was ugly by default. Some of the criticism of the show had to do with my weight, that I didn't have the delicate quality and fragile birdlike body with which Asian women are normally associated ("Cho, who is not svelte . . ."). One critic decided to be completely original and just criticize my looks ("Beauty is not Cho's strong point . . ."). Either way, they were all just passing off insults and racism as journalism.

I was working on *It's My Party*, when the prop master came to me complaining that he had seen a picture of me in a tabloid and the quote underneath said: "Margaret Cho Has Thunder Thighs." I got upset and told everybody on the set about it, and everybody got on the prop master's case. He felt bad and I felt bad; it was really a no-win situation for everyone.

He said he wasn't trying to upset me. He just thought it was ridiculous because I looked great in the picture, I looked great the way I was, and it was total bullshit that they would print something like that.

I saw the picture later, and he was right. I was thin. And even if I wasn't, the tabloid had no right to say it. But it hurt me. It hurt deeply. I was cut to the bone with every comment. One tabloid printed the "Chow Like Cho" diet, which was a fake diet that I never went on with fake quotes from me like, "When I was young I was raised on rice and fish . . ." That is so *Mulan*! It had all these recipes that used Kikkoman and almond slivers and exuberant exclamations from me like, "I don't want to be ABC's overweight Asian-American!"

The tabloids and I have long had a strange relationship. They always put me in the "Would You Be Caught Dead in This Outfit?" columns, which I adore, but then they print stories that they get from my act and try to repackage it as gossip for their idiotic readership. Facts like "Margaret is into *fisting*" would go in there plain as day—as if fisting were some sort of hot new workout like Spinning or Tae-Bo. "*Todd Tramp's now offers FISTING! Sign up and lube required.*"

That awful week before we shot the pilot, after I had put myself in the hospital, all I could think about was working out. I was afraid of losing the show by not losing enough weight. Having so much body shame and all the cultural baggage surrounding it, it's no wonder that I felt I had no other option. I did cut down on the workouts—

but only to five days a week. The pilot was finally shot before a studio audience. The audience gave me a standing ovation when I came out, but the show wasn't funny. Most of them left before the taping was over.

Then the pilot was screened for executives at ABC, focus groups, and whoever else decides what will be on the air in the fall. We all put our lives on hold until we heard the news. The big announcement of the fall schedule, the first time anybody would know what was going to happen, would be held at Carnegie Hall in New York City.

I went to New York to wait for the word so I would be close enough to go right to the event if we made it. I stayed at the Paramount and shopped at Barneys. The phone was ringing and I ran into the room to get it. My best friend, Siobhan, was with me. I picked up the phone. ABC picked up the show.

Siobhan and I ran around the room and jumped up and down and ordered room service and the door banged open with champagne and flowers. The phone rang nonstop. This was making it. The ship was coming in. It felt like my life was finally happening. I forgot about the diet. I forgot all of the executives who didn't get it. I forgot about the dumb jokes. All I wanted to do was call my mom.

It was also Mother's Day. She cried when I told her what had happened. Hearing her cracking voice on the other end made me lose it, too.

"This is the best Mother's Day I ever had. This is the best present. Oh no. There was one Mother's Day that was a little bit better. . . . That was before you born! I went to Clearlake with Daddy and we drive in mountain and when we drive there was a lot of turning kind of turning to go up the mountain kind of thing, and I get blood clot some kind of blood clot in Mommy womb—can you imagine, and we have to go to hospital, and Daddy was so mad because we have to go to hospital and we on vacation! But I don't care because I hate Daddy! And we went to hospital, and they say 'You miscarry!' and I say 'I don't know Miss Carry. Who is Miss Carry?' because Mommy don't speak English too good, so Mommy was confused! But I almost miscarry you and you almost die, can you imagine? But then we fine, and we go home, then two months later, you born! And they have party for Mommy because it was Mommy first Mother's Day and I was with you and I was so happy, can you imagine? And *that* Mother's Day—that was a little bit better."

I was invited to the announcements at Carnegie Hall. The people in attendance were all executives from the network, press, stars from all the shows, sponsors, and station owners from across the country. It didn't mean that the show would be a hit, but it did mean that we were going to be on the air that fall. We had a thirteen-episode commitment, so no matter what, we would be on the air for thirteen weeks. It felt like a lifetime. It meant that we would be given a chance. It meant that I, at least for the time being, was a television star.

I bought a black Chanel suit and a gardenia for the occasion. I rode in a brand new $100,000 white stretch limo on its first trip out. We got into an accident on the way. Tragic foreshadowing.

12

FAME! I WANT TO LIVE FOREVER. . . .

The Carnegie Hall affair for ABC's official fall schedule announcement was surreal. Stars were everywhere. Ellen Degeneres and Brett Butler were already acquaintances; I met Dean Cain and Teri Hatcher from *Lois and Clark*. I flirted with *The Commish* for most of the day. But the stars who really blew my mind were the news people, Barbara Walters and Hugh Downs. They were the most unreal. I grew up watching *20/20* like it was part of my religion, so they were my own personal icons.

After a brief meet-and-greet backstage, we were all seated in the house. There was a presentation from the president of the network and then the chairman of the network and then the Lord of the network. They were identical Brylcreem triplets. Well-preserved white men in suits and slick dick hair. They talked about "pushing the envelope," "family programming," and then—"diversity."

They showed a clip of *All-American Girl*. My image flashed on the big screen. "The first Asian-American family on television" in a booming voice-over. B. D. Wong and I looked at each other, and I could see he was crying and that just made me lose it.

It was astounding because I had never dreamed my life would take me here, so many miles from home, in the middle of show business itself, surrounded by stars and starmakers, all looking at me up there on the screen.

The way the trailer was edited made the show look a lot better than it actually was, so even though it really wasn't great, it felt like the beginning of something big.

I'd always felt strange and special, that somehow I was destined to be a star. Since I grew up without role models or even people in the media who looked like me and were doing what I thought I wanted to do, I knew that I would need a miracle.

Now, my miracle was unfolding before me, on the stage at Carnegie Hall. Everything I had ever dreamed about was happening, happening, happening. Plus, I was so emotional about every little thing because I never ate and I exercised constantly and I was so hungry and weak that I was on the verge of a nervous breakdown all the time.

I walked into the bathroom and Teri Hatcher and Brett Butler were there smoking, like the bad girls in my high school. I wanted to smoke, too, but I decided instead to go into a stall and shit a brick.

There was a big network party afterward at Tavern on the Green, a tense affair with many people standing in line to take pictures with their favorite stars. Nobody wanted to take a picture with me, so I got in line to take pictures with Dean Cain and that other guy from *Home Improvement*.

The stars of the new shows—me, Steve Harvey, and Ralph Harris— were more reserved than everyone else. We were the new kids on the block, not sure of our status. I kept wondering if we were going to get hazed. I could just see Urkel putting my head in a toilet and flushing it.

The next few days were just a blur. There were so many interviews. Suddenly, because I had a network show, my opinion about everything and anything mattered.

"Margaret—who is the sexiest man alive?"

"Margaret—can you be too rich or too thin?"

"Margaret—what do you think about what is going on in North Korea? Do you think the famine will affect plotlines this season on *All-American Girl*?"

A network person once told me that if the situation in North Korea did not improve, it would adversely affect the chances of us getting picked up for the "back nine."

We all have those defining moments in our lives, the film clips that make up our own personal retrospectives, the images that will flash in front of our eyes, should we die suddenly. I believe that at the end of our lives we are allowed to go back and make snow globes out of those defining moments. Mine is not of some wintry scene, but of one of the first parties that I had to attend in Century City for the ABC affiliates. The affiliates had sent representatives from their stations all across the country, so for many of them, this was their big trip to the city, and they were eager to meet the stars and hobnob with the rich and famous. I wore a red dress that made the old men from Peoria clutch their left arms with heart attacks.

A small band of paparazzi lined up against a black rope barrier outside, and when I walked out there with my manager Greer and my old friend Sledge, the photographers called out my name in a frenzy.

"Margaret, over here. Margaret. Margaret. Here. Over here please. Margaret you are great. Over here. Please. Here please. Margaret."

They'd never called my name before and here, it was happening. My life was happening, and for the first time, I really felt like a star. I had my purse, and I threw it to Greer and Sledge like it was a bouquet and they were my beaming bridesmaids and this was my day.

In my snow globe, it won't be snowflakes swirling around, but that little red purse, floating through the air, and me in the red dress and the paparazzi and Greer and Sledge and the first taste of dreams coming true.

There was a press conference held just before the show premiered that was specifically for television critics. Gail and Gary had been fretting about this event for weeks and they prepared me for the worst. They said the critics were going to be merciless and would ask me awful questions, and the best thing to do was to not let it get to me.

They never went over what they thought I would be asked, perhaps because they didn't have any idea themselves, they just wanted me to be ready, ready for the worst.

Sitting on the platform, with Gary and Gail on either side of me, I braced myself. The questions were relatively easy. I remember one critic, with a bored, annoyed, tired voice said, "I understand that this show is about a Korean family selling pornography. How do you expect that the Asian community is going to react to your portrayal of them as perverts?"

We didn't even bother to answer that one.

It was almost over, and then one critic asked me, "Miss Cho, isn't it true that the network asked you to lose weight, to play the part of YOURSELF, on your own TV show?"

Gail grabbed the mike from me and said, "There is no truth in that whatsoever."

I couldn't believe it. I kept looking at her, trying catch her eye, and she wouldn't look at me.

In this crowded room full of critics and TV people and photographers, I felt totally, completely alone. Another critic started arguing with Gail, and then another leapt to her defense and then I shouted:

"CAN WE STOP TALKING ABOUT MY ASS??? Please . . ."

There was a nervous laugh, a smattering of applause, and we were led out of the room. I walked, unsafe and unsure, out of the frying pan, and into the volcano.

During this period, I taped my HBO special. I wore a black pleather pantsuit, and killed. "Everything was going to be great from here on out," I thought. *Shiny shiny bad times behind me . . .*

The days at the studio were not very long, but they seemed to extend into the night and weekends because of the heavy press schedule and the fact that most of the cast members came over to my house after work. B. D. Wong did his laundry, and Maddie Corman and Judy Gold came over to watch television. I didn't see anybody not directly related to the show. My old friends and I saw very little of each other. When I pressed one of them for a reason, she said it was because it seemed I did not need her, that I had all my other Young Hollywood friends now, whatever that meant. There is much truth in the statement, "Fame does not change you. It changes the people around you." I was famous, and it made the people that I had been hanging around with resentful. Even though I don't think I had behaved that differently, I was regarded in a totally new way.

The show's premiere garnered huge ratings. There was an audience out there for us, which I did not anticipate.

Being suddenly well known was bizarre. Strangers would come up to me and start yelling what they didn't like about me.

"How come you are so fat on TV and so skinny in person?"

"How come there are non-Korean people playing Korean people?"

"How come your stand-up is funny but your show is not funny?"

I wanted so much to control what other people thought of me. One of the hardest lessons to learn was that it is not possible to do that. The problem was that I sought approval from others because I sought *definition* from others. I had virtually no opinion of myself that was not given to me by somebody else. I fought so hard to be loved because I did not know that it was possible to love myself.

A couple of Korean journalists I had befriended informed me that an older Korean woman, a colleague of theirs, had been saying that I had a clause in my contract that did not allow other Koreans onto the set of my show. She was telling people that Koreans who had been employed by the studio were immediately fired when I found out about our common heritage. I don't know why she had said this. It certainly was not true. It did not make any sense to me. Those guys may have been lying, but I don't think they were. Why did this woman have so much against me? I now understand that it is a frighteningly common thing. People of color making strides in a field run by the dominant culture tend to persecute others of their own background, because anyone else's success makes their own achievement seem unspectacular. It is a way to perpetuate the idea that race is unimportant, that it means so little that one attacks one's own kind to prove it. This is incredibly racist in itself. It is also the way we keep ourselves from really becoming strong and banding together. Worst of all, it is insidious; even accusing this woman of it, I am questioning my own motives. Am I guilty of it myself? If so, how can I stop it? Where do we stop internalized racism as far as we are aware of it?

I can only tell my story as honestly as I can.

After the journalists told me what she had said, I could not let it go. I should have let her say whatever she wanted to. I should have recognized what she was doing, but I was a different person then. These were "eye for an eye" times. Getting her phone number from the guys, not listening to their warnings, I called the woman. I left a very threatening message on her voice mail about what I had heard and told her that as a journalist, she should know better than to spread lies. I said that if she wanted to discuss it with me further she should call me. She called back almost immediately. She was furious and wanted to know who had given me that information. She was breathless with rage, and I countered her anger by making myself as condescending and controlled as possible. I told her that a woman of her age should not be so upset, that she should get a hold of herself or she might give herself an aneurysm. She hung up on me.

I was scared by how mad I could make her. I was also scared at how really fun it was, yet I felt instantly sorry. I was sure that I had really crossed the line somewhere.

A few minutes later, she called me again. I didn't pick up the phone, so she left a message demanding a written, signed apology. She spelled out her name very slowly, "in case you cannot understand the Korean." She called again and said that if she did not receive a written, signed apology within twenty-four hours that I would be "very sorry."

I spoke to the Korean journalists later. They told me she had called, demanding to know exactly who had told me what she had been saying. As far as I know, they did not stand by me. They were too afraid of her and did not want to get on her bad side.

I began to feel very alone. Part of why I had done such a thing was, in a strange way, to win their approval. I wanted them to see that I fought for what I believed in. Unfortunately, without their backing me up, it had all just seemed like a thoughtless prank.

I sent her flowers the next day, with a written, unsigned note of apology. It was not accepted.

Over the next few months, the woman used her seniority at the newspaper to compile a huge piece about the negative impact I had on the Korean community. She did not write for the entertainment section, she worked on the city news section, but she was determined to ruin me.

She interviewed many people, and I don't even know what was said because I never read it. I don't know what damage she did. Who was to say at that point? It really didn't mean anything. I already felt hated, so this just restated that painful fact. It saddened me that this was what it came to, that somebody like her would put so much work into seeing me punished, and that ultimately it was my fault for fucking with her in the first place.

It is awful that the two of us, accomplished Korean women, in worlds we had to fight so hard to get into, would use our strength so readily to cannibalize each other. I am sorry, too, that in a way, she might think I am doing it right now. I did, after many years, send her the written, signed apology.

I told her that I was a different person back then, and that I did not know who she was or who I was. I should have had the deep respect for her that I do now, a respect I gained not because of what she did to me, but because I see how much she is just like me.

I stand by her now, and I finally can say I understand the Korean.

Rejection from the Asian-American community was hard to take, mostly because the show had been universally panned by critics, panned by every major publication. It seemed like we had no fans at all, so to be deserted by the audience that we were trying to represent was almost too much to deal with.

I did not react gracefully to any of the criticism.

A friend of mine wrote a piece for a big alternative newspaper that was about how insulted he was as an Asian-American to have his life lampooned by *All-American Girl*. He felt that the show did a great disservice to multiculturalism, and that we were doing much more harm than good by our efforts. It cut me to the bone because he happened to be somebody I cared about, and my desire for revenge got the better of me.

I called him, and in as innocent a voice as I could muster, I asked him to fax me a copy of the article. He nervously asked if I had seen or heard anything about it, and I replied sweetly, "No, I haven't, but I just want to make a scrapbook of all my press, and it has to include your piece, especially since you are *such a good friend*."

To his credit, he did fax the article, then immediately followed it with a letter of apology. I did not speak to him again for a number of years. Not long ago, I called him and told him I was sorry I had put him through that. I explained that I had felt betrayed, and wasn't able to express anything but anger at that point. He told me that the newspaper had pressured him into being far more critical than he really was, for the same reasons the Korean woman felt such malice toward me.

It's interesting that at the time, I found it very easy to call up and rail against all the Asian-American critics, whereas I would never think about doing the same thing to the "mainstream" critics. I thought it was a family affair.

I read in yet another article about the Asian-American backlash to *All-American Girl* that a Korean media action leader said I was "dangerous" and that he would be monitoring the show and would be protesting at the first opportunity.

I reacted like a Korean Courtney Love. I called him and screamed totally unintelligibly about how stupid he was. This was very exciting because he got flustered right away. I went on and on about how much I had done for the "community" (nothing really at that point) and how I was being repaid with his idiocy. I hung up on him, but he kept calling me and leaving messages after that about events I could help him out with because I allegedly "cared" so much about the community. His messages were always tinged with sarcasm and a carefully concealed hatred that we reserve only for our own kind.

The most painful part of the backlash was a letter written to the editorial section of my newspaper at home. It had been submitted by a twelve-year-old Korean girl who wrote, "When I see Margaret Cho on television, I feel deep shame."

Why?! Why?! I realize now this was because they had never seen a Korean-American role model like me before.

I didn't play violin.

I didn't fuck Woody Allen.

I was just me, or actually, I wasn't even me, because *All-American Girl* was so far away from being me it was ridiculous. The first episode's story line had me doing stand-up comedy, and publicly embarrassing my family. At the end of the episode, I learn my lesson, and vow never to publicly embarrass my family again.

Quentin Tarantino, who I was dating at the time, called me up screaming, "They took away your voice! Don't let them do that! You fucking live to publicly embarrass your family!!!"

The backlash was not against me, but it felt like it. The show was not me, but I thought it was. I was not me, not by a long shot. The sudden fame, the criticism, the backlash, the diet, the schedule—it started to make me go insane.

13

CRUSH CRASH

I fell for one of the writers of the show. It was rather unexpected, but I was in a state of serious distress. The show had been on for two months, starting very strong, but with ratings that dropped week after week. The headaches and nausea from the diet pills were slowly killing me. The bad reviews and backlash from the Asian community left me heartbroken and enraged at the same time. Having no friends anymore outside of work made me question what was real and what wasn't. Finally, with the situation in North Korea continuing downhill and with no word yet on the future of the show, I needed something or someone to take my mind off it all. I found Jon.

I decided that I was gonna have a crush on him. Crushes allow us to step outside ourselves and view ourselves as we believe the crush might.

Very often, a crush is not about the other person, but about us and how we think we are in the world. By looking at this reflection of ourselves through another person, we find a way to achieve self-love without actual self-esteem, a way to admire oneself without admitting that is what you are really doing.

Crushes are about fantasy colliding with reality, the fantasy of who we think we are matched against the reality of who we are. Other people have little to do with it.

When I set off on a crush I spend a lot of time on my appearance: buying clothes, working out, immersing myself in the crush's perceived culture. I imagine I can be closer to the crush if I surround myself with the things he likes. I feel that it will rub off on me, making me more attractive in the glow of the familiar. It also serves as a way to get to know him without actually having to speak to him and risk rejection, or having him say something that might not coincide with the imagined life I have given him. I take a spare collection of facts and trivia, mix it with things he has said, fortify it with my own personal research about him, throw in a bit of profiling for good measure and there we have it—crush! *Here's one I made earlier . . .*

I needed that escape more than anything. Maybe Jon did, too, although I have trouble distinguishing what really happened with what happened in my imagination. This was not only the craziest I ever got over a guy, it was the most insanity I have displayed ever. That is saying a lot.

Jon was not handsome or sexy or particularly attractive in any way. He was having a hard time in his personal life. His mother and his uncle were both dead of cancer in the space of a week. Jon traveled on weekends back and forth from the East Coast, and he looked sad and tired on Mondays when he returned to the set.

He wanted to talk to me about things. He was leaving his job. He needed the time. His family wouldn't stop crying, he said. Maybe we could get together and talk. Maybe.

He came over to my newly rented Hollywood Hills house and sat on my red couch and didn't have much to say about anything. He felt sorry that things were going so wrong for me, too. He had the most understanding expression on his face. I don't know what he was trying to do. I hoped he had come to save me.

I was alternating between depression and denial. *All-American Girl* was on the verge of being canceled. I hated the show, and so did the rest of the world, it seemed. I had to stand behind it, because to abandon it would mean I'd have to leave myself behind in the wreckage.

It was a dark time for both of us, and the last nail in my coffin was Jon and my obsession with him. I see now that it wasn't him at all—I just needed to be rescued and he was the frog I kept kissing. I was drowning in quicksand and he was the dry twisted branch that I held onto, even as it broke off and splintered in my hand.

He was subtly persuasive in his way. There was something about him that obsessed women. It had to do with the way he withheld. He was like a geisha, or a Victorian ingenue, offering a tantalizing glimpse of his inner being. This frustrated me and many like me to total madness. I think he was proud of it.

He told me that he had once volunteered on a suicide hotline. A disturbed woman became fixated on him and he tried to break away. He had the hotline transfer all her calls. She got angry and threatened to do something bad. He did not believe her.

When she finally got him on the phone, she told him she had pulled out her eyes. The Bible said that if her eye offended God, to pluck it out, so she was calling him to tell him she had done it. She was stunned and creepily calm and not yet feeling the pain. Then suddenly, she felt it. She screamed at him fearful, primal screams, and the whole time he was trying to get her to tell him where she lived so that he could send her an ambulance. He had to talk her through it all, stand in the darkness with her. He said it was the scariest thing he had ever done.

Later, they would meet. She, of course, was now blind, and had become a nun. I thought about them meeting and how maybe she would be curious about how he looked. I thought she would ask to put her hands on his face, and he would let her, reluctantly, as he did everything.

When he told me that story, it made me feel strangely inadequate, as if my obsession with him would always pale in comparison. I wanted to kiss him when he was in my house, but he wouldn't let me. He was already cheating on his fiancée with another woman who worked on my show and he didn't want to three-time her.

What was so seductive about him was that I thought he cared about me when nobody else did. That bound me to him. I wanted him to kiss me so bad and he did and then he didn't. He pushed me onto the floor and left. That place in my house is haunted by the electricity that went through me. Later, when I missed him I would lie in that space and remember his hands on me.

Right after he left, he called from the car and said he didn't want things to be strained between us. He was sorry, but he wasn't sure for what.

He'd call every couple of months, to vaguely make plans that would never happen, or to put me off, or to be friendly, or to leave a message to call him, which he'd conveniently never be around to receive, pushing me further and further into my obsession. Days went by with me dressing and waiting by the phone and it never, ever rang. Not once.

I would keep putting on makeup and the sun would move across the sky. Finally, it would be too late for anyone to be calling or making plans, even though I thought he still might, and I would just get high and wait longer, phone by my bed. I'd fall asleep on top of the covers, completely dressed and made-up. It would be morning and the birds would be singing and I would wake with a sharp intake of breath and a realization that I had wasted an entire day waiting. The lights from the night before would still be on, throughout the house, and ashamed and desperate that I had lost another twenty-four hours of my life, waiting for a man that did not care if I existed, I would get up and do it again.

After thirteen episodes had been shot, *All-American Girl* was on hiatus, so I had nothing to do but spend my life in preparation to meet him. I went to a silversmith and ordered a beautiful flask engraved with, "Astronauts, Movie Stars, Politicians. I know you would if you could . . ."—a sort of attempted private joke that was so private that I am sure only I got it. It was a cryptic reference to the fact that I had been loved by all these illustrious men and that he would love me if he could just be as accomplished as they were or something ridiculous like that. I realized somewhere along the way that it was insane, and I never gave it to him. Actually, I never saw him and therefore was unable to give it to him. Now, I display it prominently in my home as a reminder to never let myself go so insane again.

I was so fucking crazy and I did so many drugs just to keep this fantasy of him alive. He did take me to dinner once at Off Vine. I tried too hard to seduce him during dinner, and unconvincingly licked red wine off my fingers. He said that I would have to do a lot more than lick wine off my fingers.

He took me home in his stupid Acura Vigor with the ugly sheepskin seat covers and drove me up Vine. Later in my obsession, depression, I would drive myself up Vine and feel special. What kind of life is that?

It was just like being dead, and this waiting and wanting was with me for two years. I never got over it. I heard through the grapevine that he had broken off with his fiancée. I saw her ad in the *Recycler*: "Wedding Dress For Sale $800, Never Worn, Call Reese S _____."

That set me off trying on bridal gowns like *Muriel's Wedding*. I found out that I don't look good in them anyway. What I loved about it was that everybody at the bridal boutique was so *nice*. It was the happiest place on earth: the women trying on gowns, and the women with them on the verge of tears anytime anybody came out of the dressing room. It was this joy that was so seductive. When I left those shops, I couldn't help thinking that I really *was* getting married to Jon, and it would be only a matter of time until he would realize it.

"The Wedding Fantasy" has been one of my most lasting and persistent daydreams. They go back as far as T. Sean, my blue-eyed Texan beau, from when I was just twenty. I saw marrying him in quickie Vegas fashion. Smoking a cigarette in a pink shantung silk suit, '60s style, tapping my foot impatiently, holding a tiny bouquet of baby roses in a trembling gloved hand.

Curiously, I also saw our make-believe marriage fall apart, and me drunkenly stalking him into his next relationship. I fantasized about being found by his young son from his next marriage, passed out on their porch early in the morning wearing a fur coat and pearls and nothing else, and clutching a broken champagne glass—*That's Dad's first wife before Mommy. She's having some trouble letting go. Can I call the ambulance? Please? Please? Please?*

I saw getting married to Jude, a country-western crooner I had a brief affair with, just as clearly. That particular ceremony was held in a stone church in wine country, C&W all the way down to white cowboy boots. The justice o' the peace would be Col. Sanders, and he, of course, would also cater the event. Jude would sing to me, and all the girls would cry at the romance of it all and the fact that he was taken for good.

My fantasy wedding to Marcel, my last most horrible boyfriend, seemed far more real. We'd go to the South of France, to Provence, where he had attended a wedding years before. The theme would be turn-of-the-century peasant, and we would serve stone soup. There would be fiddles and tiny flowers weaved into my unruly mass of *Manon of the Spring* hair. All the men with their black vests and pocket watches like old-time bankers would lift the heavy oak table and set it outside in the field, where we would dance and drink the night away.

I never pictured my parents at these functions because they represented the awful truth, the bad shit, not that they were awful, bad, or shitty—they were just *real*, and I could not live without lying. They were the black watermelon seeds of my existence. I wanted to just have what I thought were the good parts of my life, seedless and sweet.

I got deeply into this fantasy, thinking I could go to 1900, that expensive boutique on Main that is open by appointment only, just to price antique cotton, to see what a dress would be like should this fantasy come true. I didn't want to lose my head about my wedding dress as many a young bride is known to do. There were so many new magazines to buy—*Bride's* and *Modern Bride* and such, just like *Vogue* but with a sense of purpose and direction. The gowns in there were ugly and puffy. I realized as always I'd have to go the vintage route, or perhaps design it myself.

I thought about the bridesmaid dresses. Lemon yellow granny dresses, sort of '70s Gibson girls with big bubbly bun hairdos, which of course they'd never wear again, but who cares? Who wears anything again? I saw myself in Victoriana, white gauze and delicate white lace and daisies in my bouquet, and the bridesmaids, my friends Siobhan, Ebby, and Marcel's sister Louise, in yellow to match the yolk of the daisy.

And suddenly, it wasn't a fantasy anymore, it was outright planning. Later, when the relationship went sour and I could barely stand the sight of Marcel, I still didn't want to break up because I had spent so much time on my fantasy. In fact, I was being held hostage by my fantasy. I was willing to let myself be miserable in this relationship, to stay with someone I hated, someone who tortured me every time he looked at me, talked to me, or touched me. I was going to endure a lifetime of hell for the pleasure of ONE IMAGINED DAY!!!!!!

No matter how hard it is, I am not going to fashion a wedding fantasy for my next crush. I will stop living life for a future happiness that does not and may never exist. I will live for now and stop wasting my time. Every moment I live can be as beautiful as a fantasy. Every second of life is precious. I vow to stop wasting my time on these dreams that turn my life into a nightmare. I vow to live, to be mindful, to pay attention to life and hold it hard to my heart. Every beat another second going by.

It was so hard then to not want to lose myself in the lacy, white emotions, the soft, womanly caresses of the bridal salon. I was insane, I was being a lunatic. Trying on wedding dresses, preparing for a wedding to someone who would never even call me back. But the ladies at the boutique didn't know that. They just wanted to help me be ready for my Special Day, the one I would remember for my entire life.

I tried on a dress, which didn't look good on me anyway. I went to wait outside for Sledge to pick me up. Curiously, he didn't think anything that I was doing was strange.

I was standing on a corner of Ventura Boulevard and this guy drove up and looked at me and then went and parked his car and walked back. He started talking to me and saying that I was attractive and asked what was I doing. It took me a long time to realize that he thought I was a prostitute! Sledge came roaring up in his Acura and I got into his car and he drove my crazy ass home.

14

TALES OF THE RECONSTRUCTION

The show was under massive reconstruction. Since there had been such a backlash from the Asian-American community, an effort was made to make the show more "authentic." An Asian consultant was hired, mostly to help actors with their accents and to determine the Feng Shui on the set. It was all the more insulting because the actors didn't need any help, and "authenticity" was never the problem. It was insensitivity. The idea that there is one defining, "authentic" Asian-American experience ignores the vast diversity of which we are capable. It discounts the fact that there can be many truths, and holds us in a racial spiderweb. We were accused of being racist because we did not ring true as an "authentic" Asian-American family, when the real racism lies in the expectation of one.

Of course, the network had little time for discussions on race and culture. It was decided that the show should be moved out of the family environment into a Generation-X communal living situation. The family would still be in some of the episodes, but the focus was shifted to my life without them. This seemed closer to who I was, but it wasn't the right solution. The show was changed drastically to be more "me," but since I was never allowed to do any of the writing, and lines I put in were edited out of the final shows, it was as bad as ever.

Twenty-something angst was hot, so we jumped onto the *Friends* bandwagon. We did a few episodes where my character moved to the basement, said no to casual sex (something I would NEVER do), and moved into an apartment with two girlfriends. We even parodied *The Real World*.

Then, two of the writers were fired. Rain and Sherman were young members of the staff, and they had become friends of mine. I did not really know what they contributed to the show, as I was never allowed into the writers' room, but their sudden dismissal angered me. It made me feel powerless, though I don't understand why that did when almost nothing else had.

I used my muscle as the star of the show to get them rehired, which surprised everyone, because it was so incredibly late in the game. I just had no idea I had that much control.

It never occurred to me that I was the star.

It never occurred to me that I could have told the network that I didn't want to lose weight.

It never occurred to me that the only reason anybody was there was because of me.

The show was called *All-American Girl* and I was the *All-American Asshole* because I never realized it. Rehiring Rain and Sherman was of no use anyway because soon all the writers were fired, including a very pissed-off Gary.

I felt bad for Gary because even though the show wasn't funny at all, he really tried. He was also understanding when my diet pills would keep me up all night and I would storm into his office in a drug- and hunger-induced frenzy, making him take notes while I babbled incoherently about story lines based on *The Celestine Prophecy*, a book I had never read but thought sounded good.

The show was shot one last time as a new pilot. All of the original characters, with the exception of myself and Amy Hill, who played "Grandma," were gone. I was now living with three men, and it was "slacker-centric." The comedy fell flat, as it was all supposed to be ironic and cynical, with the humor emerging from the language as opposed to jokes.

It was an ambitious effort, and I would have to say that I did like this show, because at least it was closer to my own sensibilities. It was unfortunate that we lost almost the whole family. It is my understanding that the network felt that the Asian-American backlash to the show was so great that they lost their confidence in it. Either that or the North Korean conflict really had affected the pick-up of the back nine.

Too many Asians was what I'd imagined was being thrown around the conference room. *We'll just keep the quality Asians. The ones with high TV Q.*

The new pilot got a lukewarm response, as it was aired to a confused audience who tuned in to a show that they had become familiar with only to find entirely new characters. Everybody was disappointed, and the show wrapped without any news of renewal or cancellation.

I went home to a phone that never rang, unless it was a drug dealer I had just paged.

It was the summer of 1995 and I went to New York to play a club and settle into my uneasy future. Hanging out with friends and doing drugs was all I could manage. The many nights of Ecstasy and Jack Daniels and pot and packs and packs of Marlboro Lights really took their toll. I was having trouble performing, and one day, I woke up without a voice.

There was a signed head shot of Morrissey in the doctor's office, which comforted me greatly. The doctor injected me with cortisone, which got me talking again. A camera was lowered into my throat, much like my catheter experience, and captured on film the white dots on my vocal cords. I wished I had kept the footage of my bladder along with this. I could have done a great installation: *Inside Margaret Cho—Coming Soon—The Ass Explored.*

The doctor's orders were very clear. Give up smoking altogether. Get some rest and be careful and maybe—MAYBE everything will be fine.

Quitting smoking was one of the hardest things I ever had to do, because I loved it so much. I loved the way cigarettes looked and smelled and tasted. I loved that it gave me something to do. Inhaling the blue smoke and watching it come out of me gray was a meditation for me, an affirmation. It was a comfort, an occupation, a drug, a casual habit, a distraction, a way to not eat, a way to not pay attention, a way to not feel. I needed all these things and clung to them as I clung to life.

Even now, when someone opens a pack of Marlboro Lights, I look at the neat white rows of filters wistfully, like the old flame I never quite got over, who my heart still burns for every day.

In addition to cigarettes, I had to give up smoking pot, which was also incredibly difficult. Not entirely ready for this, I grabbed my friend Ebby and jumped on a plane to Amsterdam, so that instead of smoking pot, I could eat massive amounts of hash bon bons and "space cake," delicious confections that infused my food of choice with my drug of choice.

It was heavenly, feeling free and euphoric and insane. I was relieved not to be working on the show for the time being and lost in the idea that for the moment all I had to do was indulge myself with the tragedy of the mysterious growths in my throat and mourn the loss of my smoking life. Then, as I crammed more and more psychedelic sweets into my mouth, thinking more meant more heaven, it was just disgusting.

Being away from home helped me to think about Jon less, and for a while, my obsession lifted.

I didn't get high anymore. I just got frustrated. We left Amsterdam and moved on to England. Back in L.A., I had purchased a big brick of high-quality marijuana a few weeks before, before I knew that I wouldn't be able to smoke it. We had left it behind in my freezer.

In Holland, since it was legal, we didn't give it a thought, but now in Britain, where the laws governing it were strict, we started to miss it. Ebby and I wanted to send it a postcard: *Dear Weed: I wish you were here . . .*

To console ourselves, we drank Scrumpy Jack's cider in pubs and went up to Cambridge to watch Nick Lowe play at a folk festival. Everybody seemed to be smoking cigarettes, which made me crazy, and when we went to see *Muriel's Wedding* in Oxford, I cried for nearly three days after thinking of my one and only Jon, who didn't care about me even though I loved him so.

One day, when Ebby and I could not take the lack of pot or each other any longer, I went to a bridge in Camden Town and scored a dime bag of seedy, brown shit pot from a Rastafarian. With that dirty brown baggie, I saved our friendship for the remainder of the trip.

It's a funny thing about drug buddies. You can be tight and close and best friends, but when you take away the substance, you are left strangers. There are so many of these people in my life, people I grew up with, have known my entire life, and now that we don't do drugs or drink when we are together, I have no idea who they are. Ebby and I stayed friends through sobriety, and we had to get to know each other all over again, which was wonderful. She is a true friend and one of the great gifts in my life, but I never would have known her if we didn't love the devil's weed.

Every once in a while, I would be recognized on the streets of London, as a few episodes of the TV show had aired there, but it didn't happen often enough for me. I grew to miss the nominal fame that I had. I thought things would be the same when I got home, but they weren't.

I returned to no word on the show's renewal or cancellation. My thoughts grew darker. My management said not to worry, that the show was just a jumping-off place, that there would be bigger and better things lined up for me. Still, my phone never rang, as I divided up the big brick of pot to hand out to my druggie friends. There are few things more lovable than a former pot addict giving out her stash.

Finally, Greer took me out to lunch at Red on Beverly. In between the Paradise iced tea and Chinese chicken salad, he said, "Oh, by the way, you know the show has been canceled . . ."

I said, "Oh . . . yeah. . . ." like I knew all along, and he didn't mention it again.

After that, when I called him, he wouldn't pick up the phone, so I just talked to his assistant, who always said Greer was awfully busy, but that he'd get back to me. He never did.

Drinking eased the pain of the long nights without cigarettes and pot. I was not a good drinker by any means. My face got all red and I had to down aspirins by the handful to keep my head from exploding. My face swelled up so it looked like I had been bitten by a rattlesnake. That is why I liked to get as drunk as possible, because then I wouldn't feel myself being poisoned.

There was nothing left to do except drink as much as I could, then wake up bleary-eyed in the morning and work it off, try to wring the alcohol from my body with exercise. My managers never talked to me. My new, high-powered agents, who had been to every taping, sent me scripts and flowers every week, never called me back.

I wondered how my old agent Karen was doing. Once, I remember calling her when I was drunk, after business hours and leaving a message on her machine: "You were right about everything . . ."

Sometimes, when there was no party or gathering or comedy

show, I would get dressed up and go to Small's, this little bar on Melrose, and dance by myself. I met a guy there named Doug, who said, "You are the saddest girl in the world." I immediately made him my boyfriend.

Vodka made me unbearably honest, and I spilled out all the painful details of my life to Doug, from my sitcom cancellation to my childhood molestation by a family friend. Doug would remember everything so he could use it against me later. He'd have sex with me and say, "Am I reminding you of your molester right now?"

I did not have the presence of mind to get out of that abusive relationship. That is the only explanation I have for him. And I was too fucked up to use birth control.

Ebby and I were both late for our periods. Since we were roommates, it seemed a little strange, because we were on the same cycle. Doing our weekly shopping, we jokingly, but nervously, picked up two early-pregnancy tests along with the coffee and cereal.

I already knew I was pregnant. I could just tell. I had the odd feeling that I was not alone. It wasn't an unpleasant sensation. It was around Christmas, and I attended a party in which all the guests were on acid, and even though I wasn't tripping, I still felt altered, locked in cosmic conversation with my unborn, feeling like a little world unto myself.

I was eating a lot and gaining weight and for some reason, for the moment, it didn't matter to me. But I still didn't know for sure. I could entertain the fantasy of it, because I still thought I could be wrong.

I did my test in the upstairs bathroom and Ebby did her test in the downstairs bathroom. We screamed simultaneously "No!!!," which echoed thoughout the Hollywood Hills as both strips turned bright pink.

The reality of pregnancy was nothing like the soft dream I had

been nurturing. I could barely care for myself, much less another human being. Since I was also supporting Ebby financially at the time,
that would mean there would be four of us! I hated my boyfriend
Doug, and I was not about to have his child.

When I told him we were pregnant, he asked, "Is it even mine?"
Sure I cheated on him, but I was careful about it. He was the only one
I let fuck me without a rubber. Ah, true love.

Abortion was the only solution we considered. It was the only way.
Ebby and I made appointments at a clinic in Westwood. I was so
grateful to have her there, going through the same thing as me. It
made the situation seem slightly less tragic, and more like a screwball
comedy from the '30s—*Putting Down Baby*.

Our pregnancy tests at the clinic were definite, and our abortions
were scheduled for the following week.

In my unguarded moments, over the next few days, I felt that hazy
sweetness, the oceanic peace that your hormones give you when you
are carrying a child. It was in equal parts disturbing and beautiful. I
knew it could not last, and that was awful. I felt that something in me
was alive, and that was eternal. I imagined feeling that feeling for nine
months, to end it with the birth of a baby, my baby, and the love that
I'd have, a big, big love incomparable to anything. But then, reality
would set in. There was no room in my life for me, much less someone I would have to raise from scratch.

Inside, during that whole period, I'd felt like I was slowly dying,
and had no right to bring forth life. Still, those gentle strings of
motherhood wrapped around me, and I could feel their embrace,
and I dreamt of tiny hands night after night.

We went to the clinic early in the morning. I was quietly relieved
when we got there. After putting our names on the list, we sat in the
waiting room and silently watched the saltwater fish in the big tank
swim around.

I lay in the stirrups, and as the doctor painfully pushed his latex-coated fingers up inside me, he said, "You know, when you had your television show, I don't think they really captured your essence as a performer. If you were to do it again, I think that you should really fight for some creative control."

I said, "That's fine. Now, could you just kill my baby?"

Waking up after my abortion, that feeling was gone. I was alone once more.

A nurse came and said she had been at the taping of my HBO special and that a lot of the people from the office had been there and so they were very excited to have me in, which was horrifying but also kind of nice. I was going to offer her a signed head shot of myself to put on their wall, but I decided against it when I realized we were not at the dry cleaner's.

I felt hollowed out, as if I had been straddling an orange juicer. The operation was incredibly painful, and I thought I'd never be able to use that part of my body again. It feels like a blender is being thrust inside and turned on. I don't understand why there isn't an easier, less traumatic alternative to first-trimester termination.

Are we being punished by the medical establishment for being "fallen women"? Does the scarlet "A" we sew to our chest stand for "abortion"? I might be sad for my unborn, but I do not mourn that I could not have offered it much of a life at that point in mine. With the technology we have in our grasp, why must we still suffer? While old men can purchase their Viagra online, why do we still bleed so much?

We got small envelopes of painkillers, which I could tell right off would not nearly be enough, and our friend drove us home.

Justifying it all because of our extraordinary circumstances, I had a delicious pot relapse. We got home and settled into my red couches and ordered in a bag of pot the size of a loaf of bread. We didn't move for a month, healing, sometimes uncontrollably laughing at our hideous fortune, getting high and staying high, watching trashy movies, wondering what our kids would have been like, crying about having to kill them, and in general, having the equivalent of an anti-baby shower.

My awful boyfriend stayed away, and I was so glad to be rid of him. In times of trouble, I have always counted on my women and, of course, my gay men to get me by. I thrive on female energy, whether it comes from a woman or a man, and I am not able to function without it.

In the end, women and gay men understand longing and loss, and the pull of the physical body against the weight of societal demands. We are all witches and shape-shifters and healers and gods and goddesses, and we must stay together and join forces to lift each other up.

Gradually, I started to feel better, and knew I would have to kick pot once again. Drinking wine to help ease the loss, and buying into that weird idea that two glasses of red wine a day would lower your cholesterol, I started another deadly trend. I had gained so much weight during the pregnancy and abortion and recovery period, that all the clothes that I had stolen from my TV show didn't fit anymore.

The diet pills weren't working, so I started taking larger doses. I shed many pounds again, and got confident enough to break up with my boyfriend.

My other lover, Gaines, took up the slack. He lived in San Francisco, and I remember arranging to meet him at Tosca on a Tuesday night. I got there early with Sledge, because I never went on a date alone. I quickly downed multiple shots of Herradurra Tequila. I saw

Gaines at the end of the bar, looking tentative and tall as he always does, and I got all excited and couldn't sit still.

I excused myself and went to the bathroom for like an hour, passing out in a stall in a pool of Chinese-food vomit. A waitress came in to check on me and then soon after, I was carried out by Sledge and Gaines, past the San Francisco drinking elite, to Gaines's waiting, double-parked car. I was bruised and all sweaty and sour, a mumbled vow against Herradurra on my lips.

They took me up to the Nob Hill Lambourne, the scene of many crimes, and somehow I got from the car to the bed. I opened one eye to watch Gaines's long legs cruise the perimeter of the mattress, and he took his pants off neatly and joined me underneath the puffy comforter.

The clock read 9:46 P.M. Feeling stupid, replaying the awful memory of my head lolling back and forth in an alcoholic daze, too sick to drink more to erase it, trying so desperately to make it camp, and all these thoughts swirling in bed with him, who could have enjoyed anything?

So much past we'd had, he and I, so much history. I thought of it, lying next to him. I remember seeing Gaines in the Punchline so many years before, thinking that I had to have him, that the search was over, that it was him and that was the end.

I obsessed and tried and tried and I finally got him, but I was a mess, a filthy, drunken, disgusting mess. Miraculously, Gaines still wanted me.

Even though I was burnt out, dragged on the floor, hungover, then drunk again, uneasy, had other boyfriends, pushed him around, pushed him away, didn't call him back, decided one day to hate him for no reason, yanked his Kangaroo pin out of my jacket, lost it somewhere, forgot forgot forgot love, he still wanted me.

I think part of him wants me still. That is the miracle of him. Of his asbestos love. It was indestructible. Oh Gaines, I am so sorry. I didn't love myself then. How could I love someone as good as you?

Those days, drinking was the thing and San Francisco was a good place for it. I didn't drive, so there was no danger of driving drunk, which I did nearly every night in Los Angeles. I think my guardian angel is a crash-test dummy, who took all the hard knocks for me so I wouldn't have to. I was protected and so was the Southland, from the menace of me behind the wheel.

The only time it was really bad was the Monday night I left the Good Luck bar on Hillhurst after twenty too many Lemon Drops, and I slammed right into the side of a gang member's car. So many of them got out, it was like Barnum & Bailey's Bloods and Crips. Even though it was completely my fault, I started screaming at them, demanding to know why they hit me. I had hit them! I went off about how I was gonna call my lawyer, which is ridiculous because I have an entertainment lawyer. We didn't get any money from the insurance company, but we now all have development deals with UPN.

The gangstas thought I was crazy and left me there on the corner. The next day, feeling guilty and lucky, I found the card one of them had nicely given to me and sent him $200.

So, when I was in my hometown, I could drink without restraint, knowing wherever I landed, Gaines would be there to carry me to safety.

Sledge was easily roped into drinking with me, for he loved my wild company. We would walk up to Vesuvio's in North Beach, order two shots of tequila at the bar without sitting, slam them down, and be on the street again in the space of a minute, with a total mood change and refreshed attitude.

It was all about attitude. I had gotten to the point where I had experienced so much tragedy, I thought it couldn't possibly get worse, and if it did, then at least it would be my fault. I thought if I was going to be a failure in life, then I was going to do it in style. I wasn't just going to fail, I was going to be a gorgeous disaster.

Taking tranquilizers with my booze, I felt like Marilyn Monroe. Carried out of bars, I felt like Frances Farmer. I thought if I died this way, that drag queens would dress up like me until the end of time. If I couldn't be happy, at least I could be immortal.

15

WOODSHED

Then there was Glenn. I thought Glenn was the love of my life, the ONE, the relentless other, where I will go when I die, the glue factory, out to pasture, the zipless fuck, the Sizzler salad bar, my all and my everything.

We never even went on a date, or flirted, or had any sort of introduction to the affair. I was standing at my usual bar, a dark Hollywood place full of wine and development people. I might have been drunk, or on my way there. We looked at each other through the haze of cigarette smoke and idle conversation made while people are looking over your shoulder, and we just fell in love.

He put his hands on my legs. I just looked at them. I buried my head in his neck and breathed deeply. He was all I ever wanted. We went out to his car and made the window steam up like a clambake. I'd never had my body react to anyone so instantly. It was so natural and so easy. I pulled away from him, and it *hurt*. The only way to stop the pain was to kiss him again.

He was just another addiction, and I had already been on quite a downward spiral.

These were the days of short skirts and red wine and lots of cigarettes and the slowly exhaled declaration, "I am a creature of need . . ."

I put forth this image of decadence, eyes half closed with lust and self-absorbed angst, weaving in and out of bars and cars with a haste and hurry—when I had absolutely nowhere to go and nothing to do. I ate so little and drank to kill the hunger, so I was delirious most of the time. I was an accident waiting to happen, and Glenn was the oncoming vehicle.

Glenn was enthralled with the mystery of me, and he was just bored enough to do something about it. We met in dimly lit parking lots and shadows of clubs and alleys. We made love in the car and it didn't even seem uncomfortable. I felt like I was fifteen years old. God, when I was fifteen I was never *this* fifteen! It was exciting—he was exciting, more than anyone else had been.

I wanted him, even if he was living with his girlfriend.

After some of the initial passion wore off, when it was possible to speak without touching or have a conversation that didn't just dissolve into more fervent lovemaking, he started feeling guilty. At first it was just a little, but then, as we started to see more and more of each other, it got exponentially worse. He told me the guilt was killing him, that to sleep next to her night after night was to never stop lying, because he was falling deeper and deeper into me.

We'd started to meet at my house, late at night, and I'd turn on the pink lights and the room would glow, sexy and hot. There was a sense of commitment to it that hadn't been there in the parking lot. I felt so loved by him and so excited to feel the love toward him, and all was love, but then around 4 A.M. Glenn would always have to leave and I'd stay in the pinky light all by myself, feeling ridiculous. There was nothing to do but go into the kitchen and try to drown myself in Chardonnay.

It was the summer of '96, and the heat was unbearable—the months without a breeze, so many regrets just hanging in the air. He came around again and again, I suppose because it was simple enough to keep going. I am afraid he didn't want to know what would happen if he let me go. He saw me as deeply unpredictable. Maybe he was afraid that the depth of my passion carried a heavy price, that my rage was always close by and would one day swallow him whole, or at the very least, that I'd tell his girlfriend.

It was true that he had awakened something deep and primal within me. I would cry so much over him, painful sobs that emerged from the red, hot center of my being.

On the fourth of July, Glenn broke up with me. I knew it was coming, but I still couldn't have predicted the incredible feeling of loss. For the first time in my life, I was so upset that I was unable to eat. I wasn't eating that much to begin with, but I still thought of food with much longing, and looked forward to the next time I could indulge. Suddenly, I had no appetite whatsoever and I dreaded the thought of having to get up from my despair-induced stupor and eat. This lasted for three days. It was shocking. I started to panic and ordered my favorite foods in order to tempt myself. Turkey Reubens and pizza and Chinese food cooled and congealed in front of me. I got kind of excited that maybe I would become emaciated, but no such fucking luck. I drank all my calories instead; my daily intake of entire bottles of Jameson's and Merlot supplied me with a full day's nutrition.

Missing him, knowing that a day would end without him, no calls, nothing, was too much to bear. This longing was so familiar to me. It was the same pain I felt for Jon. He kept me waiting by the phone forever—part of me is still waiting for him, and always will be. I never fully recovered from Jon. Some people, if you are not careful, will do that to you. It was the same with Glenn.

No, it was worse with Glenn.

Glenn was a comic. I got the nightly schedule and went down to the club when he was playing. I was all dressed up, because the only thing I had to do during the day was to get ready for him. I looked at myself in the mirror over and over, not quite sure it was me. I looked at my body from all sides, confused. I looked too small, then too big. I would think I looked okay, even pretty, and then I would see myself from a different angle and be horrified at how ugly I was.

My house was hot and my air conditioning was broken, so all my makeup kept melting and sliding off my face. I'd try to put it back on, on top of slippery sweat.

We'd finally meet late at night, and since I had been thinking about him all day, and getting ready to see him for almost all that time, too, I'd be so nervous that it would take me two martinis to even be able to speak to him. I would have to be half-drunk to access my emotions in any way. Usually, I went too far, and by the time the check came I would be crying.

When we got to my bedroom, he would be filled with reasons why we had to end it, why he couldn't see me anymore. I wasn't listening. I was busy undoing his pants with my teeth. He would talk and talk, while I flew around the room, high as a kite that he was desperately trying to reel in. I always tried to find a way to force him into it, force him into having sex with me. It wasn't difficult, but it wasn't very nice, either.

I went to Washington, D.C., in the stretchy black dress I wore all the time then. I went running up and down Connecticut Avenue with Vaughn, a musician who had purple eyes so beautiful you just assumed he always had sex on his mind.

Vaughn kissed me and I didn't exactly want him to, but I didn't really mind after he did it. I kept hoping that it would make Glenn jealous; that was just not possible. Not only were we 3,000 miles away, Glenn didn't want anything except for me to get out of his life. I feel sorry for anyone that I am obsessed with. I am worse than gum in your hair, very, very close to the roots.

I beat Vaughn up with the roses he gave me, so of course, for the entire weekend, he never left me alone. Nothing happened. I was obsessed with Glenn, and nobody could cure me of it.

I went to my hotel room and I wrote a screenplay about it—the whole story of me and Glenn, and the unlikely and tragic love we shared, the story that I thought was so dramatic and cinematic. I got so wired with my own creativity that I didn't stop writing for many hours. I basically had the whole thing written in a day, and I brought it back to L.A. with a plan: If I could make this into a movie, and enlist Glenn to help me, there would be no alternative than for him to fall in love with me. Proximity combined with accomplishment was going to be my love potion, and I convinced myself of this as I typed my fingers numb.

I didn't sleep and brought the completed screenplay into my manager's office at the crack of dawn. The compulsive behavior was partly because I was so excited about the project and partly because Greer's biggest client at the time was Michael Jackson, and so he seemed to respond to me only when I was acting completely insane.

Greer loved it, and immediately started to send it out to people. He began pressuring me to write an action film. "I get it. You're a writer!" he said.

I showed the screenplay to Glenn. He loved it and was flattered, and probably terrified. I showed it to lots of people, and everybody loved it. They all wanted to help me build the force behind it to get the money together, to get it made.

Even though it was born out of this completely obsessive insanity over Glenn, the screenplay seemed like my ticket out of obscurity and alcoholism and longing and never getting. The writing was good, there was no question about that. There was truth and pain and a lot of humor in it. It could be inexpensively shot in relatively little time. It was the kind of independent film that could cause a stir. I could get all my famous friends to do cameos.

I wanted it to save me. Glenn wasn't my prince. Maybe I was my prince. *All-American Girl* certainly hadn't saved me, it just plunged me further into the abyss. I needed rescue. I thought maybe my writing would rescue me. My writing was the prince.

It would have been good to think I could save myself, but it wasn't really true. I really thought the screenplay couldn't just exist by itself. It had to be made into a movie. I would need someone to back it financially. So, I needed a producer to be my prince.

I worked on another draft of the screenplay and got all my friends together to do a reading of it at Largo. Glenn and I renewed our vows as we worked on it together in bed late into the night. I felt like Dorothy Parker lying next to him, pen and pad in one hand, whiskey glass in the other.

For a brief time, I was able to convince myself that I had it all— this new project everyone was fawning over and Glenn back in my bed. The reading was a smashing success, except for one small thing: Glenn's girlfriend came. He introduced us.

The next day, I waltzed into the offices of Traitor Pictures and sold the film to a man named Roman. The way he looked at me over the conference table scared me, but he had real film money, and a real contract. He might have wanted me as well as the film, and I tried to act like I felt empowered by it.

At some point during the meeting, it actually took hold. Roman wanted to talk about bringing in another writer to rework the script. I exclaimed, "I am an artist—I am not a collaborator!" He was impressed enough to let me do the rewrites alone.

After the meeting, I was due on the set of *Keenan*. My frenzied energy and my newfound sexual "empowerment" fueled my performance, and I got a standing ovation for talking about dicks.

I started working with Lane, the film development executive at Roman's company. She tried to teach me about story and structure, but it bored me. Her advice was not helpful, and she tried to make the story more and more conventional.

I still saw Glenn late at night, but I was losing interest in him and gaining interest in my new career as writer/director/star/ho. I went to lunches with Roman, growing increasingly alarmed by his advances toward me which were not physical, yet extremely intimate.

He called me up late in the business day, around 7, and wanted to come over and watch *9½ Weeks*. He bought me sushi and then tried to follow me home in his Range Rover. I kept telling myself that I had him under my control. I kept telling myself that I would do anything to make my movie.

My management scheduled a meeting for Roman and me at the Bel Air Hotel. We sat at a table, and he dragged my chair bumpily next to his. He picked lamb out of his teeth and worked a thread of the flesh between his lip and gum.

Lane briefly dropped in talk about our progress. She was pretty disappointed that I hadn't taken any of her suggestions with the rewrite, but she felt it was all turning out well anyway. Roman said he was making this film no matter what. His eyes never once left my cleavage.

Lane left us alone at the table to return to her Christmas shopping. Roman and I walked up to the valet. The attendants who had flirted so willingly with me before would not look at me. I felt like one of Heidi's girls.

Roman wanted to take a walk under the hotel, by the creek that ran alongside it. I sensed danger, but I tried to be as calm as I could. It happened so suddenly. It was kind of like a bear attack. I was just walking in the woods. . . . He grabbed my breast and put his mouth on it and muffledly said, "I want to be your baby."

I panicked. I didn't want this, but had I asked for it? I searched my mind for answers. He was coming at me and I had to make up my mind fast. I wanted to make my movie, but at what cost? I fucked people for a lot less, but . . . I looked at Roman's huge belly and his tiny hands, his dick that had grown huge in his baggy jeans. He had short legs, so his dick seemed almost longer than them, and it stuck out like a kickstand. I couldn't do it. Not for the movie. Not for anything. I started yelling. "No. No! NONONONONO!!!"

He wouldn't stop. He was backing me into a woodshed. I wanted to say something to make him stop. I wasn't afraid that he would overpower me. I was so much bigger than he was. I just wanted him to stop on his own. Stop the tidal wave of hands and wet mouth with lamb-in-teeth and hard dick flopping this way and that but most of all toward me—and I said, "Don't push me in there. There're axes in there!!!!"

I think that was the right incantation, because he stopped.

I went home, after he paid for my valet parking. I felt like a whore who could be bought for the price of a conveniently parked car. Nothing really happened, but it was still disgusting, and I was glad to be safe and away from him.

I didn't know what to do really. I thought I could just go on as if nothing happened, but it kept bothering me. Roman made me so mad. His interest in my project was all a ruse, just so he could get me into his fat little hands. But wasn't I encouraging it just a little? Did I have so little confidence in my writing that I thought I had to add sex to sell it?

I kept thinking about his mouth on my breast, his kickstand. I got angrier and angrier. I was going to make him pay. I turned in the next draft of the screenplay, but now with an added scene in the beginning where the lead character goes on a blind date with a short, fat monster of a man and is sexually assaulted by him. She gets away, but not until he grabs her breast and says, "I want to be your baby."

I wish I could have seen Roman's face when he read it. He was fucking pissed, but he didn't know exactly how to handle it. Lane knew nothing about us, or of his intentions to have sex with me. Roman was married with kids and didn't need anybody knowing anything.

He called an emergency meeting at the Beverly Hills Hotel with me and Lane and Greer's assistant Ched (Greer had long since abandoned me to Ched). Roman's fat little hands gesticulated wildly in the air as he went off on some lie about how he had showed the script to a "French distributor" who hated it. The "French distributor" especially hated the newly added pages about the blind date, and the unrealistic and unfair portrayal of a short man. The "French distributor" also pointed out that it was clear from the script that I hated men, and that if I were to continue in this business, I would need to rectify that.

Lane was mad because she didn't understand. Everything seemed to be going so well and now Roman was suddenly going ballistic about some fictional "French distributor." She had suspected there might be something going on between us, but she wasn't about to say anything to him or me about it. She just wanted to make the film. She wasn't too concerned with the drama that wasn't on the page. Roman was yelling at her, "If you knew how to do your job, this script would be ready now!!!!"

Lane got defensive and said, "I've been working with Margaret all this time, and she hasn't listened to me at all! Why are you blaming me?"

Roman laid it on the line that we were going to have to do another draft—"and it had better be fucking astounding, because we need it like fucking yesterday!"

We went back and forth, and I kept asking Roman, "Who is this 'French distributor' anyway? What is a 'French distributor'? Does he hand out fries or something?" Then Roman would explode again. The meeting seemed to last hours, and Ched did not say one word the entire time.

Suddenly Roman made everybody leave, except me. When the table had cleared, he turned to me and said, "How about it?"

I said, "What?"

Roman looked at me hard and said, "Let's get a room."

I said no so loud, people from other tables looked at us. I walked out of the hotel. Roman followed me. He was suddenly trying to be nice.

He said, "Look, don't worry about it. If the rewrites are satisfactory, I'll make your film."

I looked at him. I didn't know what to do. Roman took the valet ticket out of my hand. He paid the driver. I got in my car and went home feeling sick.

Lane called me that night and said, "What was that?"

I broke down and told her everything. She sighed and said, "Oh, so that's why. I can't believe he did that. I can't believe *you* did that. I mean, that whole thing between you guys happening, and then turning it in as a rewrite. It's kind of funny, but you really pissed him off. I knew he was lying about the 'French distributor.' He's not a very good liar. It's okay. I am sure we can work around it."

We tried to get it to work. I wrote that movie over a hundred times until it was completely unrecognizable to me. I took out the offending scene and added story points that felt stupid and inauthentic. I still wanted to make my film. I still needed the money to make it. I had to show Roman I was sorry somehow. I had to write my ass off in lieu of giving it to him to fuck.

The notes Roman had made were incredibly obscure and conflicting, so the rewrite became a confusing and complicated mess. I know he just wanted me to fuck it up so that when he did get around to finally saying no, he would have real reasons for it.

On Monday, Lane went into Roman's office and told him to leave me alone. She said that I had told her what had happened and that if he didn't stop hassling me, she would tell everyone in the office.

He fired her. At least that was what she said. I don't know whether to believe her now, because when I talked to her months after this whole thing, she was still working for him. I don't know what the point was of telling me that he had fired her, except to emotionally blackmail me further, to convince me that chaos followed me wherever I went.

Whatever the real story, I was told Lane was being fired because we couldn't deliver the movie he wanted. He wasn't ever going to make it anyway—he was just playing for time to see if I was going to fuck him or not.

When Lane told me the deal was off—curiously, even though she had been fired, she still made calls for him—I told her that I had expected it.

I went straight to the refrigerator and pulled out a bottle of Absolut Citron. I drank the entire thing, standing in front of the open freezer door. I didn't want to feel anything. I was afraid of what I would feel, that the pain would be so great, I would die from it. It was like when you bang your foot against the door, and you have a grace period of a few seconds, knowing the pain is coming and anticipating how bad it is going to be. I tried to get as fucked up as I could in that interim.

I felt like a failure. I couldn't even fuck my way to the top! Maybe it was that I felt worthless and betrayed and that I wrote my heart out and now I had no heart. I had done it all for Glenn, and now where was he? I guess I hadn't done it for Glenn at all, because when I started really working on the script with Lane and Roman, I forgot all about him.

I'll never really know what I felt then because I wasn't about to allow myself to feel anything but the sledgehammer of vodka and the slow death that it brings.

Roman still wanted to act like we were friends. I think he was afraid I would talk about it onstage. He left messages on my machine, trying to find out where I'd be performing. I did get around to telling the story onstage, after I had recovered somewhat. The audience was horrified and excited; they could tell I wasn't making this up. They cheered wildly for my minor victories against Roman, and mourned the loss of the deal along with me. I am sure someone told him about it, because a little while later he called to find out about the movie and if I was making it. He said that he was still in love with it and wanted to see if he could get involved in it again and why don't I give him a call when I have a chance.

I didn't talk to him for years after that. The next time I saw him, it was after this entire horrid epoch of my life. Roman came to the Westbeth Theatre Center one night when I was performing in my show, *I'm the One That I Want*, in which I talk about my experience with him so candidly.

It was Friday night and so very hot as Fridays were that entire summer of '99 in New York. It was close to the end of the run, and the place was packed. It was one of those great crowds, I burned up the stage like it was my birthright. I looked down at one point, and I saw him. I stopped dead in my tracks. Roman was sitting right there in the front row. The air was hot and humid, but I was chilled to the bone. I didn't know what to do. I was performing on so many levels, holding the audience of 250 in the palm of my hand, and still trying to stay calm even though one of them was the one I talk about as being "unfuckable."

I tried not to look down at him, but I could feel his rage rise up at me like a noxious smell. It is unbelievable, but I just carried on. Nobody could tell that there was anything different about my performance. I just avoided that part of the stage, as if I could avoid him and his anger and what he did to me. I was not going to give him the satisfaction. I was not gonna let him see me falter or fail. I would win, as I deserved to.

He moved finally. I think he went to the back of the theater. At least I couldn't see him and I could pretend to myself that he had left. I felt a little more comfortable. I thought I had made a mistake. Maybe it wasn't him after all. Maybe he still had no idea I was talking about him onstage. Maybe everything would be okay . . . I'm sure I was just paranoid. It is funny how the mind plays tricks on you and you can't figure out what is and what isn't.

Deep down, I knew it was him. Underneath it all, I felt like the entire time I was up there I was going to be shot. That Roman would just stand himself up on that kickstand and start firing away. For some reason, I pictured him with a musket.

I braced myself for the hot burning lead, all the while still captivating this audience of screaming fans. I cannot believe that I pulled it off. The show ended, and it was okay. Nothing happened. He didn't hang around after the performance, he didn't stand by the stage door, he didn't try to kill me. After all, it was okay.

Just to be sure, I hid upstairs in my dressing room long after everyone had left. I saw Roman's expression when I was up there. It was just murderous. There was blood in his eyes. He must have been mad, because when things happen to women, we are supposed to remain silent. Our shame should make us want to act like nothing happened, maintain the decorum. I refuse to be silent, therefore I become some sort of criminal.

I think if we all told our stories and said out loud what has happened to us, to warn other women, to comfort those who have had the same things happen to them, to show that we are not alone, the world would suddenly become a bigger and better place.

People ask me sometimes if I ever go too far, if I ever reveal too much of myself and later regret it. I don't think it is possible to get too personal. We all have pain. We all have doubt and sadness and horrible things that have happened that shouldn't have, and when we cover them up and try to pretend that everything is okay, then our stories are forgotten, and our truths become lies.

I tell the truth because I am not afraid to. I tell the ugliness to show you the beauty. But there is so much ugliness still left.

16

THE DRINKING CURE

I was very disappointed by the entire screenplay episode. I was very disappointed by life. It seemed like my existence was hopeless, and that everything and everyone was against me. I thought the only solution was to drink myself to death.

It was interesting when I actually decided on suicide. It seemed very practical to me. I wasn't sad about it. It wasn't a big, tragic melodramatic thing. I just felt relieved. For the first time in what seemed like forever, I was at peace.

I knew that I didn't have the courage to jump off a building or blow my head off, but I always held those as options in the back of my mind, in case things got completely intolerable. I was content to drink as much as I could until I just stopped breathing. That seemed sensible enough.

Of course, this decision to drink myself to death had been a long time coming, but now the alcohol also helped me to stand being myself for another day. I hated myself and everything I had done, and I wanted to get out, get away from me. Being drunk gave me the ability to romanticize my fall somewhat, feel beautifully doomed like Marilyn Monroe, swallowing handfuls of pharmaceuticals and red wine. I felt it would all be good for the biography someone would write in the future. That's funny, but it's true!

I still had to try to make money, so I took comedy gigs when they came along, but I was usually so drunk onstage I would have to hold the mike stand to keep the room from spinning around me. I was slowly turning into *The Rose*.

Once, at the Irvine Improv, I was headlining the show, but I had so little confidence in my ability that I brought three other acts with me—not including the other two guys already booked. I went on last and barely eked out a pathetic set while the patrons left in droves.

Too fucked up to drive back to L.A., the three comics and I got a room at the local hotel. For some unfathomable reason, I sent two of the comics to the store for more booze so I could fuck the other one while they were gone.

I don't know why I did this. I didn't even like him. He was a nice enough guy, but I wasn't attracted to him. He got on top of me and moved his fingers around inside me and kept saying, "Where's your spot? Where's your spot?" and I couldn't even feel it. It was confusing. "Spot! I usually park on the street." Or "Spot? I don't have a dog."

Fortunately, the other guys came back pretty fast as there were no stores open, and we all fell asleep fully clothed on the bed. Later, that guy kept calling me and calling me, to see if I was okay, to tell me what CDs he had in his stereo, to see if he could find my spot again. I couldn't talk to him, it was too embarrassing.

If I was promiscuous, it wasn't out of a love of sex. I tended to despise sex, ever since that first awful time. I was just using it as an escape, a way to get power and alleviate boredom, and also, interestingly enough, a way to avoid real intimacy.

Waking up with a hangover was a regular, normal thing, but the morning after the "where's your spot" incident, it was truly evil. I think that I did drugs and alcohol with such a vengeance so I could avoid mornings like those, hoping against hope that I could bypass the hangover and just not wake up. It was all part of the suicide solution.

That morning, my headache woke me before the morning light. I drove back to L.A. midday, feeling every few seconds like I was about to throw up. Getting home, I tried to ease the pain by watching *In the Name of the Father* while hanging upside down on my couch, but even the Irish struggle could not compare with the war raging inside my head. The hangover lasted well into the night, the second evening of the horrible Irvine gig, and carried over to the next drunk. And on and on.

In a way, I liked being hungover, because it was the only time I was kind to myself. It was the one time I would allow myself to eat fattening, rich foods without beating myself up about it. I needed the calories to get back on my feet again. I treated myself to big bagels stuffed with cheese and avocado, alongside massive bowls of matzo ball soup. The starch blocked the pain in my stomach and my head, and eating took away the horrible brown taste in my mouth.

After eating, I would get movies and sit at home all day watching them, imagining that I was doing something for myself, like I was attending my own film school.

Sometimes, I just had to drink in the morning to keep from being sick. At first, I tried to be genteel about it, feeling like David Niven and serving myself tall Bloody Marys, but after a while, shots from last night's bottle seemed good enough. I'd start to average two or three hangovers a day, drinking to get over the first one, getting drunk, falling asleep, waking up in the middle of the day with another one, drinking it away and getting a headache again.

Then the sun would set and the true drinking would commence, until I passed out for the night and the whole thing would begin again the next day.

I still took massive doses of diet pills, which would somehow balance out the alcohol, along with packets of Mini Thins, which were over-the-counter "pep" pills that you could purchase at 7-Eleven.

On top of those pills were sheets of blue diazepam, a kind of Valium that was obtainable in Mexico. I also had my precious prescription for Xanax, worth its weight in gold.

Wine made me fat and sicker the next day, so I just switched to vodka, frozen until it was syrupy, taken in shot glasses that were actually big enough to be highballs. I drank them freezing cold and fast, and it felt like an icicle right through the head.

I also loved tequila, Patrón being my favorite, which left a tingly purple aftertaste at the back of the throat, and a warm glow throughout my body. The bottles frustrated me because they were deceptively small, their stinginess due to a deep cavern at the base. They were expensive and I bought two at a time, getting used to the Silver, somewhat cheaper vintage, as opposed to the top-of-the-line Gold label.

Drinking in bars was an everyday occurrence, with Siobhan, at the bar at the Dresden at 6 P.M., before all the swingers came with their cocktail irony, and it was still a divey, tacky place. She and I would sit there and knock back double whiskeys and watch the news. Then we'd stumble over to Pedro's across the street and drink more and more and some nights easily put away twenty drinks each. She started having seizures at night, probably because of the massive amounts of alcohol, and had to stop drinking. I lost my drinking buddy, but not my enthusiasm, and so I kept it up for both of us, still hanging out with her in bars and watching her drink her 7-Up and telling her I missed her as a drunk.

I was in bars every evening, but my favorite drink was the one right at the end of the night, the one to put you to bed, the one to grow on. It was the reflective drink, the one that would cleanse all of the sins of the day. It was, in its own way, a meditation, a silent reverie for the day's end. I would knock back my eight-ounce shot and climb up into my antique Chinese bed and, as always, hope I died before I woke.

I am convinced I did die once. I did so many drugs one night, on top of an already-raging whiskey drunk, I floated off into a deep, drowsy place. My spirit was as heavy as hot, wet sand. I came to a dark place, filled with long shadows and narrow corridors. The walls were made of that kind of Victorian portraiture where the subject would sit next to a burning candle and the artist would trace the out-line of his shadow on the wall, making a pattern and cutting it out of black construction paper.

When people die and come back to life, they see long-lost relatives telling them it isn't their time yet, they see their lives flash before their eyes, they are enveloped in an unearthly peace, they see the behind of the universe, the backdrop of the stars, and sometimes, they see God. I see arts and crafts.

I saw my body beneath me and I couldn't get back. I tried to move my body from where I was, but I couldn't. I stayed up there on the ceiling, trapped by the shadows, terrified, trying to get my mouth to say, "Call an ambulance." I couldn't get down for the longest time, and then after a while, the fear subsided. I knew I was going to die. It was okay. I didn't fight it.

I died.

But I didn't stay dead.

I came down. I woke up in my body. The next day, my head and mouth were dry and squeaking. My salivary glands ached from dehy-dration. I was fragile as bone china, my hands shook. Yet miracu-lously I was alive.

I got high again the next night, but I couldn't get off. It was like I burned out the pilot light. I'd never get up there again.

The sickening, bloodshot mornings spread out later and later until they took up the entire day. I started doing yoga, because that was the only thing that would make me feel better. It was hell at first, getting to class, twisting into those first few impossible poses, sweating pure vodka all over the shiny wood floors. Afterward, my body would be completely wrung out of alcohol, and I could start over. Working out became not just about losing weight, but about ridding myself of the poison that I put into it every night. This is a fairly common practice, judging from the smell of perspiration in any given gym on a Saturday morning. I tried to get more out of my class by downing shots of espresso directly beforehand. This just made me want to pass out before the class was through.

Interestingly enough, even though I was dying, I was in pretty good shape. Sure, all my hair fell out, but I had a small ass. *Wow that bald chick is pretty hot! She might be dying, but a least she doesn't have cellulite!*

I liked to go to see bands a lot. Although music helped dull the pain, it intensified the self-hatred. I'd go to Largo and waste away in the back for the Friday night Jon Brion shows, loving him as much as I hated myself. The sad songs he sang were all about ghost girlfriends and how he was falling for you against his will, and I drowned in the whiskey and self-pity against the sonic love of his voice.

I ran around pop shows those days oddly obsessed with this poor singer named Bat. I wanted his attention so badly and drank fuckloads to impress him, and tried so hard to be an outlaw.

In one of the few sets that I actually did, I blasted another pop band for no reason. I said that they sucked five dicks, which is hard because there are only four of them, so one of them has to double-barrel. This is actually a really funny insult, but totally unfair because I like them. I was just showing off.

I remember weaving back and forth on my heels and swallowing an entire glass of shitty red wine from the bar at Small's. I grabbed Bat and hurriedly assaulted him with a "DO YOU FIND ME ATTRAC-TIVE?!!!?!!!" He pulled away terrified and said while he was running away, "Of course but let's just take our time and get to know each other."

Going back to visit that memory is so sickly sad, not just because of my behavior, which was abominable, but because of how I felt about myself. I was immersed in self-loathing and then suddenly struck by all these delusions of grandeur where I thought I could have any man—or woman for that matter—in the bar.

Maybe it was the dread of leaving town, which it seemed like I was always doing. Maybe it was loneliness. It just felt like a disease.

There were other, external reasons helping it along. Sledge "yessed" me into insanity, condoning my outbursts and celebrating my crazi-ness in the name of being fabulous. He spoke of us as if we were a kind of New Age Zelda and F. Scott—diving into the hotel fountains without care or repercussion, thinking we were beautiful and damned when actually we were just okay-looking and pathetic. There is a part of me that worships my former recklessness. If only it were not so sad underneath. If only it did not have such a rotten core.

I suppose most of it could be put down to grief. I was mourning the loss of my TV show, my grand and massive and very public pro-fessional failure. I felt unattractive and fat no matter what I did. I was still hopelessly in love with Glenn, and he did not love me. I had tried to climb out of it with my screenplay, only to be demolished by Ro-man and my own stupidity. I thought that everything I did turned to shit, and that my future was closing in on me fast and I had no-where to turn. I thought it couldn't get any worse, and then my grandfather died.

My grandfather was a minister, and offered me my first glimpse of show business. In his robes, he looked holy and taller than he was. I loved how he held parishioners in the palm of his hand when he spoke, always with a smile on his face. He was at times oddly distant and then completely in love with my brother and me. He spoke English better than most of my other relatives, and was eager to practice on us when we were around. He never went outside without a hat, and even though he was badly scarred around the head and neck from a terrible fire many years ago in Korea, he was still very handsome.

His health had been declining for some time, and my mother left frequent updates on his condition on my answering machine. "Hi— is Mommy. I want to tell you two things. Number one. Grandpa is going to die. I don't know when he gonna die. Mommy just tell you now, so when he die—you not surprised. But you don't have to tell him. That's not nice! And he know already. Number two. Did you get that shampoo I sent you? I send you shampoo that is good for the fine hair! You just use a little bit, and don't use too much! You just use a little bit, and lather and rinse—but don't repeat! That's wasting. You don't have to repeat!!!! To review: Number one. Grandpa is gonna die. Number two *(beep)*." The machine always cut her off before she could finish.

I did not see him very much over those last few months. Mostly, the situation terrified me. I had not really been close to my grandparents since I was a child, but my fondness for them was beyond words. It's just that during my troublesome teenage years, a huge chasm developed between me and my family, and later, through laziness and self-obsession, I never bothered to build a bridge back to them.

The last time I saw my grandfather was at my grandparents' tiny apartment in Japantown, where they had used a walk-in closet as a prayer room, a telephone booth to God, a little sanctuary that my brother and I would hide in when we were small.

He was lying on the floor on a heating pad. He was so thin and frail. He looked up at me and his eyes were glassy and dark blue. He grabbed my hand and held it hard. I waited for his grand farewell, some lasting words of advice before he left this world, a piece of him I could keep in my heart forever.

"What happened to your TV show?!"

He fell back and shut his eyes, and slowly released my hand. I never spoke to him again.

We went home and my mother apologized for the fact that the funeral director was coming over. "I know that it is kind of early, he not dead yet, and I hope he can live longer but it is better to prepare—then we don't have to worry later." She talked of burying him kind of like packing a picnic basket. "So we can save time and beat the traffic."

I hid out in my teenage bedroom and read the lipstick graffiti on the mirror in front of the closet. "I belong to Prince." "I love Duran Duran." "Adam and the Ants rule the world."

The funeral director was in the living room with my mother and suddenly he started screaming. "It's her! It's her! So that means you must be MORAN!!!!!" He was quoting my stand-up act where my mother screams my Korean name, and my mother started doing it, too.

My mother called me to come downstairs ("MORANNN!!!!") and the funeral director, a big Chinese queen, starts up again. He'd recognized my photo on the mantel and had switched gears from staid undertaker to screaming teenage girl in seconds flat.

After a few minutes of gushing and shy shuffling of feet and stammering by me, they went back to discussing the burial plots and funeral arrangements. "I am sure this is gonna wind up in your act!" he said brightly as he was leaving. The entire episode was shockingly morbid and embarrassing, but it really made my mom's day.

My mother is not just the gateway of life to me, she is the one for death. As my grandfather lay dying, she tenderly cared for him, with quiet efficiency and grace. The rest of the family fell apart under their selfish grief, but she hung on, boiling the rice, crushing the pills, driving to and from the hospital, laying cool hands on old, soft skin.

I remember how she had beamed when he died, her phone call joyous and tired and glad that he was gone and suffered no more. She seemed almost like a midwife with her weary but ecstatic voice. I saw that in caretaking, she had found a certain calling and purpose. It was the job that no one else wanted but that she took gladly, just like the white rubbery fish eyeballs that lay on the massacred carcass of grilled fish, that the rest of the family had left behind.

At the funeral, before they closed the casket on my dead grandfather, she kissed him and kissed him. He was cold and wooden and so dead, but it was still him. She wasn't scared or sad or anything; she was just love. I tried to copy her, but as close as I could get was touching his hand, which felt like plastic. He was hard and hollow and I had to shudder, even though I loved my grandfather so very much. I cried awful choking sobs from so deep inside that it hurt coming out. Still, I was horrified by him, by his deadness, by his open-casket state, his horror-show-quality makeup, his eyes and mouth sealed forever, how it didn't look like him but was unmistakably him. I saw my mom as more brave then, and closer to him than anyone had ever been. She had helped him die. She gave death to him as she gave birth to me. She was wondrous to me then. She is always wondrous to me.

I remember my two aunts at the cemetery, walking up to bury my grandfather, tiny and thin, and my mother marveling at it. "Your auntie say she stay slender by eating very slowly then everybody eat and so she don't like to sit by herself so she just finish just like that and how can be like that? I wish Mommy can be like that." But that day, they were so frail they had to hold each other up just to walk up the path.

There was a really old lady from our funeral party walking around the gravestones by herself. She had this mad dowager's hump on her back and she was bent almost completely over. I thought, *This is her hood. And she's about to pour a forty on the ground for all her dead homies.* She cleaned up the trash that blew across the graves.

I thought of dreams that I'd have where I'd be running through the cemetery. I couldn't get out and I would run and run and the stones would be endless and relentless underneath behind in front of above me. I would be drowning in some kind of marble death. I didn't have that feeling, even though I was just as surrounded by graves, as I watched my little bird aunts trudge the path.

A friend of my father's drove up, and my escort Sledge told him he'd left his lights on. He smiled, even though Sledge is white and Koreans rarely smile at white people unless they are buying something, and turned his lights off. My father's friend went up to my aunts. He told me he's known them their whole lives. My one aunt says about the other one, "She was once the baby. Now she is an old lady." He says, "She's always a baby to me." And I thought, sometimes flirting can be heartbreakingly beautiful.

That trip, out of respect for my grandfather, I tried to quit drinking.

17

ROOM SERVICE AND RALPH

This was not the best idea. During the service, my hands shook and my mouth was dry. I was mourning and withdrawing at the same time. A black dress and a nice case of the DTs.

I held out until that night, when I went to meet friends at a café. One of them remarked that I looked like I needed a drink. That was all it took. I had only a glass of white wine to keep off the sickness, but I was drunk the next night and then the next and I did not try to quit again for a very long time.

Some mornings would be so bad that I would swear off alcohol, really meaning it for the few hours that I suffered. Usually, it would be when I had to travel, and the blinding headache and sour taste made it hard to negotiate different time zones and altitudes, not to mention early flights and coach-class service.

One day, the sickness was so bad, I thought I really meant it. It was the tail end of a big trip playing many dates across the country. The last night was to be in Monroe, Louisiana, at a university not far from New Orleans.

I arrived in such a black mood, my bloodstream slow from all the residual drugs and alcohol. Checking into the hotel, my energy was renewed with all my thoughts of sobriety and health. I attacked the salty hotel exercise room with zeal and enthusiasm. With every step on the StairMaster, I felt better, and drew closer and closer to a clean and sparkly future.

The auditorium was filled to capacity with 800 teenagers. The first act, a cowboy comedian, had them on their feet by the end in an appreciative standing ovation. This seemed like a good sign. It was not.

When I walked out onto the massive stage there was incredible silence. I don't think they knew who I was. Maybe they thought I was a teacher. My first few jokes got a polite response. Then, I lost them. That sounds a bit mild actually. "Lost them" implies that I had once *had them.* I didn't, and I couldn't *get them.* It got very, very bad.

Jokes that usually got hearty laughs and applause just came out of my mouth and stood almost visible in the thick air. Suddenly, a mocking laugh came from the depths of the auditorium, and the whole crowd responded to that! They were laughing at the guy laughing at me.

Then the boos started. Howling wails came up from the crowd, and every time I would try to speak another mocking laugh would interrupt me. Pretty soon, it was a symphony of jeers and boos and hyena laughs and a mass exodus of teenagers from the auditorium. In the darkness, I could see only the outlines of their legs. From the distance, it reminded me of when ants had overtaken my sink one hot summer, and the teeming, glossy black throb of legs, of so many ants and just one of me. It made me feel faint in the same way.

I could not leave the stage. I could not accept my defeat gracefully and walk off. This just made things much, much worse.

I was on for so long trying to reason with the mad crowd, they had organized a sing-along of *"Na na na na, na na na na, h-e-he-hey— good-bye!"* in the round.

I endured this for more than half an hour, several minutes over my scheduled time. I left to a rousing standing ovation, not because they had enjoyed me, but because they were weary of hating me and were so relieved that I was gone. The headliner went on and killed.

Backstage, everyone that had been so friendly earlier, students that had brought me to their school and now held my $8,000 check, would not speak to me or even look me in the eye.

Two female students stood by my limousine and cried hysterically, saying they were fans of mine and were so traumatized by the experience that they felt they needed to apologize to me on behalf of the state of Louisiana.

I drove back to the hotel, with the cowboy comic going on and on about how he would never stand for such humiliation. I, oddly enough, did not seem to find it humiliating at that moment. It was surreal. It was devastating, but I wasn't embarrassed. They never even gave me a chance. There was nothing I could do, except piss them off by doing all of my time and not leaving until it was over.

The night was such a crushing blow to my ego, even though I wouldn't admit it to myself then. I hadn't been booed off the stage for more than a decade. It didn't seem possible to me. I was a successful comic, I'd already paid my dues—didn't they know who I was? I felt I had failed everywhere and that standup was the last thing I had to turn to—and now it seemed like that was gone, too, just like my TV show, just like my screenplay, just like my grandfather. There was no way I was going to let myself feel that despair. I knew it was coming and I had to do something. I was bracing myself for the pain. I wasn't feeling it yet, it was like I was experiencing a brief amnesty. I was delaying my misery, until I had some liquid relief. Obviously, this was a bad night to decide to quit drinking.

Quickly, I called room service and had them send up four shots of tequila. Normally, I would have had the booze already cooling in my room. There would have been multiple shots laid out neatly on the table, the tops of the glasses covered with magazine subscription cards, awaiting my arrival. But, I had decided to quit drinking earlier that day, and since the Holiday Inn had no mini-bar, and I was too ashamed to drink in the bar by myself, I was lucky that room service was there and ready to take care of me.

I belted down the shots quickly and felt festive, and much better about that evening's performance. Perhaps it was just a fluke. It would make a great story to tell back home. There was joy in my voice as I called room service again and ordered more tequila. The waiter regretfully informed me that the bar was closed and apologized before hanging up.

I panicked and searched my luggage for any loose Valium, an errant Xanax or Percodan that might have fallen out somewhere. As I emptied my purse, there was a knock at the door. It was the room service waiter, off duty, still in his bow tie but now wearing a leather bomber jacket and an "I'm off work" grin. He had a bottle of Jose Cuervo 1800 in one hand and Styrofoam cups in the other. What could I do but invite him in?

He was cute in a sad Southern way, and he told me all about his gay/lesbian theater group while we drank the rest of the bottle. We discussed Edith Wharton and how terrible Monroe was to live in, especially for queer readers. I told him how miserable the show had been, and he was not surprised at all. Drunk, I called up Sledge in California and had him join the party, with me on one line and the waiter on the extension. I don't remember anything from that point on, so I must have passed out on the bed with the phone next to me.

I woke up late the next day. I had wet the bed, but I was too hungover to care. I just rolled to the dry side and fell asleep again. I awoke much later with only half an hour until my flight back home.

I cried repentant, shameful tears as I shoved my piss-stained clothes into my backpack. The clothes smelled oddly familiar, much like my childhood, and I felt like I was dying all the way to the airport.

I realized that I could not stop drinking. I realized that I really was going to die.

That room service waiter called me a couple of weeks later. I had trouble placing him at first. In truth, there had been so many room service waiters, so many people that I had shared this sort of debauchery with, it was hard to remember and put names and faces to all of them. I had always been fortunate, throughout my reckless drinking career, to land in the company of polite and considerate gay men. They were my guardian angels, taking care of me and being happy to do so. They make me believe in God, and they make me think that God is gay.

In my selfishness and my tendency to black out all the time, I never bothered to thank any of them or try to contact them again, and time and distance has now made that task totally impossible. He was such a nice guy, though, and I think about whether he is still there in Monroe, Louisiana, if he is with the same boyfriend that he loved so, a kind of forbidden love in the South, much like the outlaw romances of Wharton's New York, and I wonder what the gay/lesbian theater is putting on this season. If I could suggest something, it would be a drag queen rendition of *Annie* called *Trannie*. "The sun will come out, tomorrow . . . *bitch*." That would really piss those kids off.

Things felt better at home, which they always tended to, at least right when I got back.

One day, I inexplicably and rather impulsively drove down to the animal shelter. I love dogs. I wanted one so badly as a kid that I composed a written proposal to my father on the virtues of *Man's Best Friend*, a contract outlining my duties as sole caretaker of afore-mentioned "*Friend*." The document contained many extras, such as promises to get good grades from then on, a clean bedroom, a new-found interest in prayer, and a television boycott.

My father was so impressed that he let me have a dog. We adopted an unruly shepherd mix from the SPCA, and he died of mange before he was a year old. My mother loved him even more than we did. She cried on the bed so long and hard when the vet came and took him away to be put down. She screamed out his name—"Lucky! Lucky! I am so sorry Lucky!" I thought it was really unfortunate that he was named that. I will always remember his sweet, stinky-dog smell, and my eyes teared up to smell it again at the animal shelter.

The West Valley Animal Control Center is a scene that can only be described as "Doggie Death Row." The dog's faces are so long and sad, big eyes staring out at you from behind the bars, knowing their fate, knowing that your taking notice of them is unlikely. The older dogs seem hopeless and depressed, the young ones, wild and un-aware, fighting over themselves to get to you.

There was one cage that looked empty, then I walked past it and thought I saw something move. I stood in front of the bars, and a tiny dot appeared out of the shadows. The dot moved toward me. It was a little puppy, not much more than three pounds. He didn't look like a dog at all, with his short snout and tiny legs. He looked more like a bear cub.

We stared at each other with wonder. He bit the bars of the cage, presumably teething, but I interpreted it as him trying to get closer to me. He was beautiful and magical, the way baby animals always are, but had a large wound on the top of his head. It bled between his ears.

The volunteer took him out of the cage. She said he'd had an infestation, but that he was a good dog. I held him. He was so soft and small he scared me. His eyes were brown and limitless. He looked at me with such love, it was hard to put him back. The card on the cage said he was not available until 7 A.M. the next morning. I asked if he had any brothers or sisters. "No. He's all alone." Just like me, I thought.

That night, I went to the Buddha Lounge, a gay Asian dance club, and listened to Erasure all night, as my friends cruised rice queens on the dance floor. I drank Cosmopolitans, and visualized myself dancing with my little bear, lost in a cosmic waltz until the end of time.

The next morning, I got up late and hungover (of course). Panicked, I headed straight for the shelter. The little bear wasn't in his cage. I went down the long row of unwanted and abandoned dogs, some barking, angry that I wasn't stopping, some sad and crying, some silent, with their back to the bars, resigned to their fate. The dogs, once they come in, have only four to seven days to be claimed or adopted. If nobody comes to rescue them, they are put to sleep. They are not dumb animals. The most heartbreaking thing about it is that *dogs know*. They know where they are. They know they are going to die.

At the end of the hall, there was a large cage filled with squirming puppies. My little bear was sitting quietly in the corner with his eyes closed. His head seemed worse. The wound had opened and was bleeding again. All the other dogs stopped attacking him to come say hello to me as I stood in front of the cage. My heart leapt, and I asked for my bear to be taken out.

I held him in my arms, and he tried to wriggle free. We went into the office to get acquainted. He was tiny, I don't think he was more than six weeks old. He was black, and his tiny paws were tan, like he had boots on. He marched all over the desk and tried to grab a French fry from one of the volunteers.

The volunteer petted him. "Look at those intelligent eyes." He had such a thoughtful expression. There was so much pain there, too. "You've seen so many terrible things," I said. "You're so little and already the world has not been good to you." I wanted to cry and cry when I looked into those intelligent eyes because I distinctly saw myself. I knew if I could love this dog, I could learn to love myself.

Just then, there was a big commotion in the shelter office. An old, sorry-looking poodle had been dropped off by an old, sorry-looking woman. As soon as the woman left, the poodle started to wail—an indescribable, horribly painful sound. The volunteer said, "That dog is being left here. The owner is having her put down. She knows what is happening. She knows her owner is having her killed. What a shame. Nobody is gonna want that dog. It is a crying shame. People have no respect for life."

The poodle continued keening, and peed all over the floor. The volunteer asked me to take my little bear outside so that he wouldn't be upset by the highly distressing scene. I stood out in the cool shadows of the concrete building and held my tiny one in my arms. He looked up at me with reverence and wonder, quiet, not moving, just letting himself be held. I looked into his big, puppy-dog eyes and said, "I vow, from this moment on, to give you a beautiful home. I am going to take care of you and love you forever. You are going to be my child, and I will be your mother. Because I have respect for life. Your hardship is over. You went through all that so we could be together. I will never forget that." He fell asleep right then. I fell in love right then.

I put him in a box and drove home. He seemed frightened at first, trying to get out of the box, whining pitifully. I had to stop every few seconds to keep him from getting out.

At home, I immediately put him in the sink and washed all the blood and fleas out of his fur. Wet, he was the size of a hamster. He hated the water, but I washed him until it ran clean. I dried him off with a kitchen towel and set him down on the floor.

Tentatively, looking back at me constantly as if to ask permission, he stepped onto the great expanse of gray carpet. He explored all the little corners of the room, gaining confidence with each step. I think he understood what was happening, started to feel secure right from the beginning, like he could feel my love, knew it was real, and ran with it.

He plopped between my two massive platform shoes and fell asleep.

I took him to the vet because he was sleeping so much. At first, I thought it was cute, and knew that puppies tended to need lots of rest, but this dog seemed narcoleptic. The kind vet took one look at the dog and said, "How much did you pay for this dog? Can you take him back?"

"Why?"

"Because this dog is going to die."

Great, I thought. We'll just die together.

I named the dog Ralph, after Ralph Fiennes, because he is my favorite leading man. *The English Patient* had just come out, and I was playing nursemaid Juliette Binoche to my poor injured doggy, Ralph. I was measuring out drugs every hour and resting my head on his chest while listening to his stories about the big, mean world, the sad he saw, the bad he saw—the madness and the kibble. I also liked the idea of saying his name every day, over and over, with the odd pronunciation—"Rafe." Ralph slept in my lap, and I drank bottle after bottle of Absolut and slept with him. He wouldn't eat or drink. I had to take him to the vet so they could inject him with fluids. The staff at the animal hospital just looked at me sadly every time we came around.

This gave me the excuse to stay home around the clock. The

stand-up gigs I was getting were few and far between. I'd spent too many nights onstage in a blackout. It was starting to affect my reputation. The Monroe show was also such a crushing blow to my ego, I felt like I'd somehow lost my ability to do stand-up. I thought about retirement, nursed my dying dog, entertained Glenn every once and again, and tucked into my own waning existence.

18

MARCEL

Through a rather boring chain of events, I met Marcel. He was living to die. I was years long dead.

Marcel loved me from afar for years, once proposing marriage when he barely knew me. "What a great way to get acquainted. It might work! Marry me first, then we can sort out the details . . ."

I found it extremely charming. He didn't pay a lick of attention to Ralph. When Marcel would come over, Ralph would try to stay awake as long as he could, maybe because he knew that I wouldn't be crying into his fur. Instead, I cried into Marcel's fur. It's sad, but I never loved Marcel. He was funny and nice, but I wanted a distraction from Glenn, who had become so inaccessible. I wanted to punish Glenn by being with someone else, by attempting to be self-sufficient. Glenn had made me so angry by staying with his girlfriend and still loving me out of turn. It was not fair, and I returned the unfairness, not to the sender but to Marcel.

I wasn't attracted to Marcel, but that had never really been an issue with me in the past. Most of the time, I felt so ugly that whenever I received any male attention, I felt obliged to return it, even if I didn't feel anything. I had this ridiculous notion that since I wasn't really worthy of love, should some accidentally come my way, I should not pass it up. What a terrible way to live your life, and that is how I was for most of my teens and twenties. Even now, if someone I don't particularly fancy decides he wants to get to know me, I will take the time to call him or talk or even go out on a friendly date—and I will still feel guilty if I don't sleep with him! At least I'm better than I used to be. (*"Maybe if I give him a blow job he will shut up . . ."*)

What does it take for us to start to value ourselves? I believe it begins with talking about it, sharing the pain, shedding light on it, so like shadows, it fades away in the brightness.

Marcel was in love. He kept telling me, "You just *know.*" He told everyone he knew that he *knew.* It was suffocating, but I think I was looking for a faster way to die; the one I had chosen was taking way too long. Also, I got into all the plans Marcel wanted to make. It gave me a direction, because I'd been so disillusioned by my career. His way sounded so appealing: marry Marcel, move to New York, have a baby, and order leather armchairs for Pottery Barn for the rest of my life. Have my kids say, *Did you know Mom used to be a comedian before she met Dad? Isn't that weird? Yeah, she got pretty good actually, but she gave it all up so she could have us . . .* They could bring press clippings from *Entertainment Weekly* for show-and-tell.

So what if I didn't love Marcel? So what if I used the interesting things he would do in bed as cannon fodder for my estranged lover Glenn. It seemed like a good idea, and I believed that it was, even as I kicked Marcel awake on bleary, hungover, pre-dawn mornings so he could go do community service.

Marcel had been court-ordered to do twenty-four days of community service with the Hollywood Beautification Team for getting drunk and falling asleep in someone else's Mercedes. My groom, Goldilocks.

He was a terrible alcoholic, just like me, and it is also just like me to judge him. I really shouldn't. What a crime it is to pretend you are in love, and the pain it causes visits upon you tenfold. It was all for selfish reasons. I wanted a convenient way out of the mess I had made of my life. I wanted a new career—even though I loved the old one, I was just too fucked up to do it anymore. I wanted revenge on Glenn. I wanted someone to understand. I just wanted. I couldn't possibly give.

Fantasy and denial were my favorite pastimes, and combine that with drinking, self-obsession, and outright stupidity, it is quite easy to ruin your life. I was unhappy, and wanted a way out of it. Marcel was there, willing, in love. It was convenient.

Poor Marcel. His only crime was loving me. He talked incessantly of his ex-girlfriends, and I became jealous, not because they had been with him, but because they were not with him anymore. He was desperate for me to meet his parents. I *had* to. There was no avoiding it. Being as close to him as they were, I can't understand why they were so nice to me. Couldn't they see in the way that I looked at him that I didn't love him? How could they not see that their son drove me crazy? Where did I learn to be such a liar? Maybe it was Marcel's need to be doing something, to be planning something, to have this bright, shining future and someone to hang it on. He talked constantly of love, how we were in love, how one just *knows*, how I was the *One*, how he *knew* I was the *One*. He spent so much time talking about this love that we were in, I have yet to know when it was happening. All I know is that we drank. Night after night, entire bottles of Patrón and Absolut, countless glasses of Merlot, vodka martinis and bourbon straight up—there was no end. Then, horrific, bloodshot mornings, where I would fight off throwing up while he talked about our love and college friends of his that had died.

Ah, love. We all hang so many hopes and dreams and expectations on it, like ornaments on the Christmas tree of dysfunction, with the shining star of inadequacy right on top.

In the midst of this disaster, we cleaned up a little, packed up and went back East. There were the snapshots taken of me and Marcel at his parents' house in Florida. I am red and flushed from the heat and the booze. The pictures are stiff and he and I look fat and uncomfortable in them. That day I had gone with the family to the "whites only" country club his parents belonged to. Even though they themselves were not racist and were silently horrified by the club's policy, it did not bother them enough to boycott it. They gave much money and time to this place, this anachronism, this relic of the antebellum South with apologies and tight smiles to me.

I wanted to go there out of sheer curiosity and a punk rock hope of actually getting kicked out. Marcel wanted me to go but then fretted and fretted over what I was going to wear, making me change out of my T-shirt and shorts into a Lauren button-down oxford and J. Crew khakis which were dirty but acceptable to him anyway.

I could tell he was quietly nervous but didn't know what to say or do. I didn't want to play golf with him and his father and his father's oncologist friend, so I stayed by the pool and swam laps in the hot rain. They didn't kick me out, but there was something wrong. It was subtle, but loud as guns.

The mothers pulled their kids away from me, as if they feared I would steal them and teach them how to stir-fry their vegetables. I kept swimming in the pool to avoid them, staying underwater where my race was not as clearly defined. Then I thought even doing that would arouse comment *(They can hold their breath for a long time, on account of they gotta go pearl divin'! See what I mean?).*

I emerged starving and hoping that I could order a club sandwich from the cheery-cheeked staff that serviced the families around the pool area. They all avoided my gaze, bestowing sleazy, self-conscious smiles on every other person around the pool, everyone except me.

I was not imagining this. I could feel it.

There was an hour to go until Marcel would be back. I sat up stiffly in the pool chairs, miserably waiting, staring at the servers, daring them to look my way. They were even more efficient than usual, as if to taunt me with their efficiency, handing out menus, taking orders, lifting up huge round trays filled with steak fries and little hotel bottles of Diet Coke, asking all the whites if "everything was okay."

I was indignant and ashamed. I kept thinking, *I am almost white. I am just as good as white. I am off white.*

I plotted a million revolutions and forms of revenge in my head. I thought of blasting the servers when I was on Letterman, in my couture dress and with my new movie project. I saw them cringe as they watched from their lumpy futons in their studio apartments with broken air conditioning in the middle of South Florida, ruefully recognizing me, confronting their own racism in the night, and the juxtaposition of my glorious media life and their damply innocuous, anonymous one. I saw me asking point blank for a menu, being refused, tossing the big, tan one, the girl with the heavy eyebrows who looked at me the least, into the Olympic-size pool, black satin bow tie and all. I was so wrapped up in my fantasies that I almost didn't notice Marcel standing right in front of me. "Hey are you okay?"

"Yeah. I'm starving. Let's go."

I should have just asked for a menu. I should have just acted like I belonged there. I should have just broken up with Marcel right on the spot. I didn't do any of those things. I just kept my mouth shut, tried not to drink too much, held my breath until I got home.

When we had been there for several days already, I checked my messages at home. My video store had called informing me that I had not returned some tapes: "*Beaver Fever* is late. Please return it as soon as possible."

Before we left, we rented some porno videos to keep me from passing out when we did it. Since we had different flights, because I was coming from work in another city, I asked Marcel to return the tapes. He failed to do so, so now my video store thought that I was unable to return tapes on time because I couldn't stop masturbating.

I got off the phone and Marcel and his father were standing right there. I started to tell Marcel what happened, not saying what the video was, of course, and he got angry and said, "You can't expect me to follow through on that shit. Don't you know me by now? You cannot rely on me."

His father joined in. "My son is totally incapable of doing anything for anybody else. That's m'boy." They laughed a good long laugh, and I fell irretrievably in hate.

As much as I hated him, I hated myself more. He didn't really do anything wrong. He was just human, yet I couldn't accept that. *How dare he love me?* I thought. *Doesn't he know how worthless I am?*

I didn't know how to get away from him. I didn't know how to get close to him. I drank and ate to try to chemically erase his presence. When I was loaded and full, he just loomed larger, wanting to have sex with me.

He'd stopped drinking before, but he was back with a vengeance. Being sober had made him totally unhappy, so now he lived in utter pursuit of happiness.

When we got back home, we experimented with not drinking.

One night, we decided to try to have sex without alcohol. I was terrified. I had never done it sober before in my life. He lay on top of me and a torrent of emotion swept over him, the usual stuff ("so in love . . . you are the one . . ."). I, on the other hand, got cold and stiff. *I cannot feel anything. I cannot love anything* went through my mind over and over. I tried to go to sleep and forget about sobriety. He ended up drinking.

We had a hellish cycle, drinking away our relationship troubles and emotional barriers, growing closer in the high, then waking up, hungover strangers. Most mornings he had to go do community service and would come home in the afternoons totally wrecked, angry and demoralized and wanting to get fucked up as soon as possible. We had decided that since the Hollywood Beautification Team's HQ was just minutes from my house, that he should move in with me. These plans all sounded fine when we were drinking. It's just that when I could come home after a hideous day of auditions, with pot smoke and loud alternative rock billowing out of the windows, to a man I hated who was pumping iron in my living room, it was almost too much to bear.

We didn't get along, but he convinced me we did. He made me think that I had a fear of intimacy, when in reality I just hated his goddamn guts.

He'd tell me that I had a fat stomach and that I had to just deal with the reality of that, that my body image was distorted and that I was putting myself through hell because I had a fat stomach.

He told me angrily that he'd hoped I would gain twenty pounds, at first acting like it was a joke, but then really acknowledging it for the curse that it was.

He borrowed $500 and never paid me back.

Marcel, Marcel.

I put up with it because I didn't think I deserved any better. Marcel was nicer to me than I was to myself.

Siobhan's birthday party was where it all came crashing down. We had made a pact not to drink that day, and when we got there, he broke it. He was so insecure, feeling like he was being judged by all my famous friends, that he went right for the beer, getting louder and louder with each one and looking at me with silent guilt and defiance. I was so angry that I decided to keep my part of the bargain, just to spite him, just to show him I could do it and he couldn't, just to be superior, even though I could feel the gears in my brain grinding together.

We had to stop the car on the way home because we were fighting so much. I half-heartedly accused him of flirting with my friend Jane at the party, and he overreacted, which made me madder because it convinced me that I was right.

In a rage, I bought two bottles of Patrón while the car was stopped. We got home and immediately drank one. Things got calmer for a few minutes.

Marcel wanted to get high and he couldn't find his stash. After much searching, we finally found the plastic bag, empty on the floor. Poor little Ralph had eaten the pot!

Marcel chased Ralph all over the house, threatening him, asking him mockingly if he was high. The dog was so weak and frail anyway. I actually feared for his life. I started to scream at Marcel, and he acted like he was just kidding, told me not to get angry.

"Why—did you really think I was gonna do something? C'mon babe. What is happening to us? I'm not gonna hurt your dog. I was just kidding . . ."

But I didn't think so.

Ralph hid from us as we drank the other bottle. We passed out on the bed not long after that.

In the morning, when we woke up, the bed was wet. It was not an uncommon occurrence, but this time, the stain was in the middle. We couldn't figure out who wet the bed.

I thought, WHAT KIND OF FUCKED UP MÖTLEY CRÜE *BEHIND THE MUSIC* BULLSHIT IS THIS??!!!!

I was sick of myself. I was sick of living this way. I was sick of dying.

I realized I did not want to die.

I wanted to quit drinking.

Most of all, I wanted to get away from Marcel. Why was I doing this to myself? Why was I doing this to him? Why was my life such a mess? How am I going to get out of this one?

Marcel could see that I was serious about quitting. About getting sober. About living. He went into the kitchen and opened all the bottles of expensive wine and the rest of the Patrón, even the stale Sapphire gin and Pimm's from Wimbledon parties of yore. He ceremoniously poured them all into the sink, and I cried as if my life was going down the drain.

I saw a new side to Marcel. He was so glad that I was getting clean that he did, too. He became my rock, my steady, what I relied on to get me through those tough, early nights.

The hangover of the last few years did not go away for a couple of days. What I noticed first, was that time seemed to go by much more slowly. Then, I learned how to fall asleep instead of pass out. I noticed that when I worked out, my sweat did not burn my eyes.

Early sobriety was wondrous, and the newfound purity made the constant battles with Marcel subside. We went to New York and walked the streets holding hands in the hot city night. I thought he'd saved me, and I hung onto him like a life preserver. It was all so romantic. Without alcohol he was a changed person, full of love, reason, and unlimited strength. He was handsomer, sexier, a better man.

I played Carolines and I found a renewed sense of enthusiasm in my work. Audiences found me funnier, more alive, happy. Sometimes

I had drunk because I thought I hated my job. I realized then that I loved my job, and that being fucked up all the time made me hate it because I couldn't do it properly. It was tiring though, and at Carolines, where multiple shows a night were the norm, my energy reserves were low.

On Saturday night, Marcel invited his many friends to the show, and had them all come backstage to meet me in the tiny dressing room. My throat hurt and I was exhausted, so when I had to entertain all his friends and be the gracious girlfriend between the 9 P.M. and midnight shows, I couldn't help but be a bit reserved.

There were like ten people in the small dressing room, which was only about eight feet wide, and which also served as the staff locker area and restroom, not to mention a greenroom for the other comics. None of his friends would leave, and Marcel kept making me talk to them, when I wanted to just kick everybody out and break the mirror and slit my wrists with the shards of broken glass.

Marcel could see that I was annoyed and didn't know how to deal with it. To make him feel guilty, I tried to appear as exhausted as I could. I think that I have the same ability as some reptiles to change their skin color to fade into their surroundings, but for me it is not as much to fit in as it is to manipulate others. I made big dark circles appear under my eyes. This made Marcel really mad, so he took all his friends and went drinking at a nearby bar.

"Well, since you are so tired, I guess we're going to go have a *drink*." The word hung in the air for a second, his secret way of getting back at me. I registered it, wanted a drink myself, decided I would be superior and above it, watched him leave the dressing room with all his comrades, and did the midnight show with a sore throat and a nagging feeling in my gut.

He came to pick me up after the last show smelling beery and remorseful, so I let it go.

When we got back to L.A., Marcel had decided to move back to New York, assuming that I would be coming shortly after. I couldn't wait to be away from him so I could get out of the cycle of self-abuse, so I wouldn't have to be around him anymore. Still, it never occurred to me to break up with him. Perhaps I was afraid that I would have to admit to being wrong about him. Afraid that all my wedding plans would go down the toilet. Afraid that I would have to tell all my friends that we weren't getting married after being so convinced that we were. I'd also miss all the attention that couples who are presumably in love get. Everybody assumes that love is the most enviable state, because happy, young couples are the building blocks of families, which are the gateways to the future. People look at you with admiration. When talking to anyone I didn't know very well, I'd mention Marcel—my fiancé—and they'd always stop the conversation momentarily to congratulate me. I'd see the faraway look that some women would get, the envy, delicious and cold. I was not so willing to give up that privilege, no matter how much it cost me. Everybody thought I was so lucky. I was sure that I would see it someday.

We came back to L.A. because Marcel still had many days left on the community service chain gang. He was afraid he might have to go to jail because he had taken so long to complete his sentence. As usual, I would kick him awake, bargain and plead, until he got up, took huge bong hits off the water pipe made from a wine bottle, and went on his way.

Luckily, he completed his sentence without a hitch, and made plans to return to New York. I counted the days like a prisoner, and soon, it was time. He was depressed and angry, running red lights all the way to the airport. When I dropped him off at the curb, he cried like a baby. He was going to miss me, he said. Things weren't going to be the same, he said. I should hope not, I thought, but I didn't say it. I drove away with my heart doing somersaults in my chest. I was crying too, not out of sadness but out of sheer joy and the delight of freedom. I came home to a clean and empty house, with no trace of him except some shirts he had left behind. I held my skinny, shaky, sickly dog and felt whole and new.

I wasn't going to New York. I told Marcel so over the phone shortly after he left. It took all the courage I had in me to do it. It was the first act of me finally looking to save myself. I didn't even know I was going to do it. I had been making out a "to do" list. There were things on it like "Return videos, dry cleaning, drop off Ralph at the vet . . ." and at the bottom, without even realizing I had done so, I wrote, "Find the strength to leave Marcel. . . ."

I couldn't believe I had written it. It terrified me. I crumpled it up immediately, before he could have a chance to see it, afraid of his finding out that I was cheating on him, with myself. But after, I knew that I could never go back, and that even though he called every night and would talk for hours about love and plans, that his days were numbered.

After he left, I felt much calmer and happier. It was easy not to drink. I didn't need to block anything out. Since I had been getting high every day for all of my adult life, being sober was an altered state unto itself. I never felt better in my life, and now with Marcel gone, I was ready to fly.

Still, his late-night calls came daily to clip my wings. It had to end somewhere. I had finally let go of the wedding fantasy. I started to see that the reason I had always been so miserable was that I constantly put everyone else's happiness before mine.

I went to New York to visit Marcel, mostly to end the relationship, but I got so caught up in plans. We had tickets to *Rent*, an invitation from Bobby Flay for dinner at Mesa Grill. Christmas was coming and I'd already bought presents . . . everything was so inconvenient, who had time for honesty? He was still driving me crazy. Sometimes, I was so exhausted being around him, that I would fall asleep spontaneously, like a narcoleptic, and wake up hours later, stuck in the nightmare.

He had made a strong effort to get clean after our last time together, and now, because he was sober and had no other fixes, he wanted to have sex with me all the time. There was no way I could do that. He repulsed me physically, and I would practically shrink from his touch. The few times he wore me down with his bargaining and demanding, I jerked him off, and could hardly hide my grimace.

I came back to L.A. still in the relationship, and not sure where to turn. I couldn't keep doing this to myself. I couldn't keep doing this to him. I couldn't keep doing this to love.

I went to a yoga class on Larchmont and stood on my head, thinking inversion would shake loose an answer. It did. I discovered that there was a goddess deep inside me, standing around my heart like a wallflower, waiting for me to ask her to dance. I saw that whatever I had in front of me, I could use her strength, instead of mine, to lift it. She agreed to be my power plant, which was such a relief, as I had been running on empty for so long. When the class was over, I was afraid the spell had been broken. I wasn't sure if it had been some massive *Lillias and You* hallucination. I wanted it to be true so badly. I knew that I could not leave Marcel without her strength. I knew that I could not leave the hell I had made for myself, unless she was there to give me a ride.

I cried and cried and tried to stop crying briefly as I went into the supermarket. I got as far as the deli, and I got number 99 and they were only on 57 and I fell apart.

An old woman in a plaid coat and snowy white hair came up to me and offered to trade numbers. "I got 70, if it'll make you feel any better. . . ."

"No—it's ooookkkkkaaayyy. I'mmmm fiinneee . . . realllyyy," I choked out between sobs.

"That's okay, honey. Take it. I've got all the time in the world."

Totally embarrassed, I turned away.

She just kept standing there, holding out her white ticket.

"We have a while. Do you want to tell me what's the matter?"

I didn't want to. But I felt the need to justify my crazy appearance, crying uncontrollably in yoga clothes, at the glass deli case at Mayfair Market, and so I did, as fast and as plain as I could.

"I have to break up with my boyfriend, but I just feel so *guilty*."

She just stood there, holding her ticket.

After a long pause ("58! . . . . 59! . . . . 60! . . . . ") she said, "Oh, honey. I felt so guilty, I married him!"

"61! . . . . 62! . . . . 63! . . . . 64! . . . . 65! . . . . 66! . . . . 67! . . . . 68! . . . . 69! . . . . "

I took her ticket. How could I refuse a goddess?

When I drove up to my house, I could hear Marcel on my machine, leaving a loud, long message. I ran in the house and picked up the phone. I told him that I was leaving him, that I didn't love him, that we could not get married. I told him not to call me anymore. He hung up on me. I held the phone for a minute longer, not believing what I had just done. Not believing, not believing, then finally, believing. The red light was blinking on the machine, and I looked down at it and punched Erase.

Marcel was not that easily persuaded. He called and called many times after that, but I never spoke to him again. The calls finally stopped coming. I hear through the grapevine that he is doing well, and I wish him nothing but the best. I am not trying to hurt him in writing this. I only want to tell what happened, how I felt. His family was very kind to me when I visited them, and there were times when I really did think Marcel was my only friend in the world.

When you finally turn on the light in the cellar, among all the cardboard stereo boxes and old shoes you want to throw away, you see there are still treasures you want to keep forever. I have taken all the barbs and thorns out of his love and kept just the blossoms, dry with age and remembrance, and pressed them in the book of my heart.

19

ON THE MEND

Just after I left Marcel, my old agent Karen called me. I was so glad to hear from her—we hadn't spoken for years. She had read my script and loved it. I told her everything that had happened with Roman. She couldn't believe it, but then, of course, she could.

She said that whenever I decided that I wanted to take over the world, she would be there. I believe that when you take those first steps in loving yourself, the universe conspires with your soul to keep that love affair going. I had taken baby steps in sobering up and leaving Marcel, and now I was ready for a quantum leap.

There was still Greer to contend with. Actually, it wasn't even him. He had left the company, but before leaving, had me sign a three-year contract, binding me not to him, but to his old firm. I was being handled by his assistant Ched, who once told me "The Asian thing puts people off." What is the "Asian thing"?! Some gimmick that I pull out of my ass every couple of years to jazz up my career? Like I am Steven Seagal.

Getting out of that contract wasn't easy, partly because I was afraid. How did I know what was going to happen? How did I know who to trust? I'd been through so much heartache with my career, it was hard to imagine it getting any worse. For the millionth time in my life, I had nowhere else to turn.

Karen still had utter confidence and faith in my talent. She booked me at countless clubs and colleges, and I fell in love with my work in a way I never had before. I realized that when I was onstage with the mike, I was home, and that when I am at peak performance, when the crowd is right, the night is relatively young, and God is there, nobody does it better.

I wrote constantly and toured with a vengeance. Karen came with me for all my gigs, taking notes, helping me rebuild myself. Siobhan came and opened for me, which made those road trips more fun than they'd ever been before.

I recorded a new comedy CD, with proceeds benefiting the Montrose AIDS Clinic in Houston. It felt good to do something for myself and help others at the same time. I started to feel useful. I started to feel good.

We traveled together like nuns, from city to city, and the planes and trains and town cars that had once been so lonely now felt like raucous road trips, the stuff of independent films.

Siobhan and I wrote and produced a sketch comedy show called *The People Tree* at Highways in Santa Monica while keeping up a hectic tour schedule. I was rejuvenated by work and by being clean for the first time in my adult life. My stand-up started to change with me. I wanted to do more than just tell jokes for half an hour a night. There was more I wanted to give.

I started to talk about my experience with the TV show, something I had avoided in all the years following it. I didn't want to bring it up, I didn't want to be seen whining about failure, I didn't want audiences to think I was that same person. I was ashamed of what had happened, so I tried to pretend it didn't exist. Being silent for so long had rotted my insides, but when I began to speak, all the misery and despair dissolved. I began to see that my experience was horrendous, and also incredibly funny. There was so much to say, I almost didn't know where to start.

This was the birth of my show *I'm the One That I Want*. It came out of my club act that I was doing at the time, where I wanted to share what had happened to me during my long absence from the public eye. The show covered my television experience with enough emotional distance to make it funny, not depressing. It also explored weight issues in greater detail than I'd ever gone into before. My attitudes toward my body were changing.

During the first few weeks of sobriety, I lost a lot of weight, mostly as the alcoholic bloat receded. I was still taking the diet pills, which I had stood by for over five years, even after they made my hair fall out.

When my body got used to not drinking, and I ran out of pills, my diet "doctor" mysteriously vanished, leaving L.A. without a trace. I couldn't face another shady "fly-by-night-devil-may-care" medical situation, so I started to gain weight, which was terrifying. This time, however, instead of embarking on another insane diet, I thought, *Fuck it. If I am fat, then I am fat. Fuck it. I am going to eat whatever I want and see what happens.* I realized that I didn't have to be thin to be acceptable to any network, or to get a job, or to please Marcel, who was as demanding of my figure as I was. All I had to do was be happy.

So I ate everything I could get my hands on for the first few weeks, appetizers and dessert with every meal—even breakfast. Then I just forgot about food. My weight went up, and then slowly started to go back down. This time, the thinness I acquired was not attached to the usual baggage.

Before, I would lose weight and then suddenly experience a flood of male attention, not necessarily because I looked better, but because I *thought* I did. So then, I would find myself having sex with people I didn't want to be with, thinking I had to be grateful for the offer, never refusing anyone since I could not afford to let this body go to waste. I had worked so hard and starved myself, I felt like I had to store up all the sex in some sort of "fuck bank" in case I got fat again. The underlying message to my psyche is horrifyingly clear: "You have to be thin to get love, but the love you get is not enjoyable, so you suffer this self-hatred, just to make room for a different kind of self-hatred."

Subconsciously, I was terrified of being thin, so I would sabotage every plan by overeating, and then punish myself with exercise, and then get too hungry to control myself around food, and on and on and on.

So one day, I just dropped it. Fuck it. Game over.

I look better today than I ever have.

Don't kid yourself into thinking weight issues are not important. It isn't a frivolous thing. Fat is still a feminist issue. Weight is not just about our bodies. It's how we feel about ourselves. It affects every decision we make. The status quo would like you to think of it as a petty, unimportant thing, to make fun of it like it is a ridiculous, female obsession, a weakness. It is one of their greatest weapons. Don't become a casualty. This war is almost over, and we are going to win.

When we let go of that, our arms are free to do everything.

It's not easy at first. You have to completely dismantle all your thinking, the way you see your body, the way we all so casually grab parts of ourselves and say, "I hate this" and "I need to get rid of this." We need to stop taking exercise classes named "Butt Burners" and "Saddlebags 101." We have to stop buying magazines that scream on the cover, "Get the body you want now!" We have to stop living our lives with the dressing on the side.

Once you start, you will never go back. Like Gloria Steinem says, "We need nothing short of a revolution." Join the ranks. Aunt Sam wants you!

Accepting myself was like getting to know a new friend. It was amazing to buy clothes that fit me instead of ones that "will fit me in a couple of months provided I stay on my diet." I had beautiful, stylish things that I could wear anytime, instead of ratty, everyday, pilled, faded, Lycra leggings and sweats, the only things that fit me from a closet filled with expensive pants that were so small that I couldn't get them over my knees. I gave away as many of those unworn dreams as I could, hanging on to some pieces just in case I had kids. I made room for my brand-new life.

Trading in my emotional baggage for a slim suitcase filled with new clothes, I moved to New York and started a run of my show.

I opened *I'm the One That I Want* at the Westbeth Theatre Center in New York in June 1999. The house was packed every night, right from the beginning, and the press schedule, along with getting used to doing so many shows every week, made it an exhilarating ride.

I remember being interviewed on a morning news show and discussing weight issues. The anchorwoman exclaimed, "That's ridiculous! You're not *that* overweight." I snapped back, "I'm not overweight at all! Your attitude is the problem." She ignored my comment and went on with the interview, but when I watched it on tape, they had cut that part out.

People are stupid and will say what they will say. It's not just weight, either. It's everything. The challenge is learning not to give them the power to dictate how I will feel about myself. Learning how to love myself from within, to make my opinion count the most, knowing that no one and nothing is going to save me except myself—these are the lessons I have been forced to learn. That is what my life now is all about. That is why I have written this book.

I met people over the entire summer who told me they loved the show. So many women who also worked in the entertainment field said they had gone through similar experiences, and hadn't had the courage to talk about it. They thanked me for my honesty and strength.

The gay men of the West Village were so kind to me. One guy sent me a basket filled with Vidal Sassoon hair care products, and it was really beautiful, but then I opened it up and it was all for dry, damaged hair. Thanks, bitch.

I danced on a float for the Pride Parade, and got carried all over the place by shirtless young men.

Finally, for the first time in so many years, I felt good. I was happy. I am happy.

As I got better, my dog got better.

He is as tall as me!

We go everywhere together. People talk to you a lot more when you have a dog. I was walking him one night and this homeless guy jumped out and said, "That dog gonna wind up in a pot of rice!"

And he probably wouldn't have said that if I was by myself.

20

WHAT IT'S ALL ABOUT

I'm the One That I Want had such a successful stage run in New York that I was able to launch a forty-city tour. Every performance was sold out, and I made a feature film of it at the Warfield in San Francisco.

I premiered my film at the Honolulu Gay and Lesbian Film Festival. The audience was terrific, and they gave the film a standing ovation. It was thrilling, yet I was completely self-conscious. The film was a labor of love, and I am as proud of it as I am of my stage show, but seeing myself up on the big screen still takes some getting used to.

There was a brief Q-and-A afterward, which was not too painful, except when one man asked me if I still gave good head. I explained that even though I did not give as much head, it was still good, as I felt it was a matter of quality over quantity.

At the reception afterward, I spoke to a young Japanese man I had met a few months earlier during my run at the Diamondhead Theatre in Honolulu. He brought pictures of us together with his lover Tim, who had since died of AIDS. I remembered meeting them at Hula's on that trip, where I was making a special appearance.

Tim had looked so frail and thin, it did not surprise me that he had passed away.

This couple had made a strong impression on me—they were not like the rest of the rowdy, party crowd that usually hangs at Hula's, Honolulu's most fabulous gay hangout. Yutaka, the Japanese man, had presented me with a beautiful ribbon lei, and Tim had laughed about how he had spent the afternoon furiously sewing it in time to give it to me. I hugged them both, we took lots of pictures, and we all left at the same time. Walking out to the car, Tim told me how much he loved my work, especially the film *It's My Party*. They got into their Honda Civic, which was parked in the handicapped space, and waved to me as they drove away. Watching them, I was moved by the great effort they had obviously made to come see me that night. I took the ribbon lei home and placed it on my altar. Dedicated to love, the artifacts collected in this shrine are reminders that I am loved and loving.

The night of the premiere, Yutaka had me sign his pictures of the three of us "To Tim and Yutaka." He put a letter in my hand, bowed, and left.

I got back to my room and read the letter. Yutaka wrote that when he met Tim, he had been very afraid of AIDS and didn't understand anything about it beyond that fear. Still, he was so in love with Tim, he decided to move to Hawaii to be with him. They had a difficult five years together because of the complications from Tim's illness, and because of Tim's mother. Already upset that Tim was gay, she was even more unhappy that he had chosen to be with a Japanese man.

Tim told Yutaka that he was a fan of mine, and that I did a lot of work to help gays and people living with AIDS.

Tim's health grew worse, and he kept his spirits high by listening to my CD on the way to the hospital. He especially liked Track Six, *Racism Affects Me in a Really Stupid Way . . .*

I felt so honored by that. Whatever successes I have had, that is the single one that I am most proud of. He listened to me on the way to the hospital, and it made him feel better. My heart wants to burst out of my chest at the thought of it, the idea of the unseen strands of love that connect us all to each other. Our ability to help someone when we are not even aware of it. I just want to live in the helping, to devote my life to it.

Yutaka wrote that Tim was thrilled about meeting me at Hula's and that even though he coughed a lot during my show, it was still one of the highlights of his life. He was so glad that he was able to do that before he died.

He said he couldn't yet accept Tim's death, and that he still expected to go the hospital and see him, smiling the lover's smile at him. The city was filled with memories for him, of all the things he and Tim did together.

Even though he was still learning English, Yutaka wanted to write a screenplay about his life with Tim. He wrote that if one audience member agreed with and understood his story, then "That's enough successful our meaning of life."

He ended the letter with a poem to Tim:

I need tears more than ocean
I need smile brighter than ocean
I need sleep deeper than ocean
I need voice like ocean

I think about Yutaka and Tim all the time. That I have touched their lives with my work makes me feel like "That's enough successful our meaning of life." There is joy inside the deepest sadness, and that is what life is all about for me.

I never would have met them if I hadn't survived. I never would have made that CD if I hadn't stopped drinking. I never would have known about love if I hadn't tried for once to love myself. When we are able to love ourselves, we open the door to more love. So much rushes in. So much rushes out. Never underestimate the power that you have in the world. After meeting such remarkable people, I know that I never will.

Acknowledgments

Special thanks to Karen Taussig, Christopher Schelling, Elizabeth Shara, Dr. Nicki Berke, the kids from SHAME, Peter Borland, Ralph Raymond Cho, Mabel Jackman, Georgina Taussig, Lorene Machado, Edward Jackman, Mayra Gomez, Richard Rushfield, C. Gibbs Review, Ebby Parker, Bruce Daniels, Karen Kilgariff, and Hahn Earl Cho.

© Tim Courtney

About the Author

MARGARET CHO was born and raised in San Francisco. She currently lives in Los Angeles with her dog, Ralph. In 1999, Margaret's one-woman show, "I'm the One That I Want," received *New York* magazine's Performance of the Year Award, a MAC Award, and was named Great Performance of the Year by *Entertainment Weekly.* In 2000, the self-produced and self-distributed movie of the same name garnered its own impressive reviews and accolades. She is also the recipient of the first ever GLAAD Golden Gate Award, honoring her as "an entertainment pioneer who has made a significant difference in promoting equal rights for all."